Praise for *Paranormal Confessions*

"*Paranormal Confessions* is a wonderfully creepy book. After spending a few nights at the Bellaire House and experiencing the spirits within its walls. I can say it's very haunted and still has a few secrets to share . . ."

—**Johnny Zaffis**, paranormal investigator

"There is no better tour guide to the mysterious and highly haunted Bellaire House than Kristin Lee. In *Paranormal Confessions*, Lee takes us room by room, from attic to underground tunnels, recounting the house's history, introducing its ghostly inhabitants and sharing her own experiences and encounters. *Paranormal Confessions* is a deliciously shivery book."

—**Judika Illes**, author of *Encyclopedia of Spirits*

"Intriguing and educational, *Paranormal Confessions* is a fascinating compendium of the many types of entities, both benevolent and malevolent, that may inhabit a location—or even a person, as with parasitic attachments. Writing expertly from her direct experiences, Kristin Lee scrupulously explains not only the many signs of paranormal activity, but also the causes or reasons that hauntings may occur. Most impressive are her helpful hints at the end of each chapter, which include brilliant protection techniques to avoid both spiritual and physical harm. *Paranormal Confessions* is now part of my personal working library and will be used as a reference guide for years to come."

—**Miss Aida**, author of *Hoodoo Cleansing and Protection Magic*

T0026400

"I have investigated locations for thirty-five years. I have been to places that are terribly frightening and some that are quite benign. The Bellaire House is a location that I will always hold dear to my heart.

I was able to witness firsthand the activity that Kristin writes about in her book, and, without hesitation, I can tell you that Bellaire House is one of the most active haunted locations that I have ever investigated. I was honored that I was asked to perform the Minor Rite of Exorcism and help my friend."

—**Bishop James Long,** exorcist and bishop for the United States Old Catholic Church

PARANORMAL
Confessions

TRUE STORIES OF
HAUNTINGS, POSSESSION & HORROR
FROM THE BELLAIRE HOUSE

KRISTIN LEE

Foreword by Andrea Perron

HAMPTON ROADS

Cover design by Kathryn Sky-Peck
Floor plans by Steve Amarillo / Urban Design, LLC
Interior by Debby Dutton
Typeset in Adobe Garamond, Cardo, Gill Sans and ITC Garamond

Hampton Roads Publishing Company, Inc.
Charlottesville, VA 22906
Distributed by Red Wheel/Weiser, LLC
www.redwheelweiser.com

Sign up for our newsletter and special offers by going to
www.redwheelweiser.com/newsletter.

ISBN: 978-1-64297-026-5

Library of Congress Cataloging-in-Publication Data available upon
request.

Printed in the United States of America
IBI
10 9 8 7 6 5 4 3 2 1

Dedicated to all those searching for answers
from beyond the realms of one dimension,
into the past, present, and future.

To supernatural researchers and
investigators who are discovering the
spiritual and metaphysical aspects of life.

In tribute to the legends of the
Heatherington Family.

In memory of the spirit of Patricia Krivenko,
"Grandma Honey."

Contents

Acknowledgments

To my husband, Daniel Hough. The Bellaire House Research Team: Jeff Taflan, Rebecca Gardener, Mike Simpson, Layne Krivenko, Kat Lang, Bishop James Long, Carrie Forgacs, Jon Campbell, Allison Welly, Susan Curtis, Sheri Imer, Nichole Wilson, Brandy Kerstetter, Jim Backus, Aaron Shriver, Landon Wells, Eddie Hill, Renee Rodrigues, and Miguel Cantu, Jonny Blaze, Ashley Blaeser, Michael Muench, and the Paranormal Confessions Crew.

Thanks also to Kellyann, Rett, and Steven Huff; Mike McCallister; and Maria Schmidt.

A very special thanks to my Mom, Patricia Korpon, Judika Illes, Greg Brandenburgh, Jim Chase, Jennifer Parker, Mike Parker with Royalty Maintenance, Pitch Black Paranormal, Southern Illinois Paranormal, SIC In The Shadows, Wes Coleman, Richard Estep, Rob Saffi, Travel Channel, Bellaire Police Department, and all the teams that have investigated Bellaire House.

Foreword

I understand the fascination with the paranormal. Having grown up at the now infamous haunted farmhouse in Harrisville, Rhode Island, I have seen the dark side of existence and I know the sensation of being watched and followed, leered at, and imposed upon by spirits or entities who make their presence known without reservation. Their sense of entitlement is certainly warranted. They never require or request permission. After all, it was their house first, and I suspect the same holds true for Bellaire House.

Perhaps it is this kind of familiarity which explains the immediate connection I felt with Kristin Lee from the moment we met. As kindred spirits, we were instantly drawn to one another. It was unspoken, implicit magnetism. I did not know her back story, nor did she know mine. Instead, it was a certain *knowing* as our eyes first locked—we embraced as virtual strangers who knew each other well. At the time, my film *The Conjuring* was still nothing more than a script, a developing screenplay. The third book in my trilogy *House of Darkness House of Light* had yet to be published, and Kristin hadn't read either of the volumes already out in the world. Ours wasn't a "worldly" reunion. A netherworld simpatico is a more plausible explanation for the instant attachment that formed between us, one which could not be denied or ignored.

Over the years we stayed in touch, Kristin and I maintained relatively close contact belied by the occasional phone call or a post on social media. A few words exchanged here and there did not begin to express the engagement. Because of my rigorous travel schedule, it took more than six years for me to make my way to her neck of the woods, at her insistence! As we approached Bellaire House I sensed an eerie uneasiness. Though I had seen numerous pictures of the place, it wasn't that kind of familiarity. I had recognized the back roads of the route we took, yet I'd never been there before. Based on the number of historically haunted locations I've visited, I learned a disquieting lesson long ago: forewarned is forearmed. However, even though Kristin had informed me of the history of the house to a certain extent, it mattered not. I was ill-prepared for what I encountered there.

Of course, the beauty of Bellaire House's antiquity is what first captured my attention. It is nothing less than lovely. Hardwood floors, a fireplace tough to glance away from, and innumerable charming qualities impossible to overlook, it is authentic to its historic past, retaining elements of its original splendor. Yet, within a matter of moments of entering the house, every hair stood up on my body as a shiver passed through me. A spirit passed by. The shadow figure caught in my peripheral vision did not want me there. Feeling unwelcome and a little sick to my stomach, I did not have to say a word to Kristin. The expression on my face said it all. She took me by the hand and walked me toward the formal parlor, as if we could exit the existence of my tormentor. He followed us. Admiring the baby grand piano, I ignored the sensation and made light conversation with several of the investigators who were there to set up equipment for the paranormal event. It wasn't enough of a distraction. He hovered over me as if to intimidate, and it was effective. Before long I had to excuse myself and go outside for a breath of fresh air. Over the course of two days and nights, that became my coping skill, my modus operandi—come in, engage, walk outside, and breathe. Goodness gracious, the evil resident was oppressive. There is no doubt in my mind. It was male and it was offended by my presence. It did not want that house inhabited by me or anyone else arriving for the event. Suffice to say, the grim presence I immediately encountered is the most formidable force to be reckoned with, and he was by no means alone. Actually, I got the distinct impression that the spirits there would prefer to remain undisturbed, resentful of those who trespass on their turf and seek them out for reasons of their own. As others conduct historical research and subsequent investigations of the property, the more that is exhumed and revealed.

If you are an aficionado of the supernatural, curious, and eager to experience the darker side of existence, Bellaire House is a necessary destination. If you never get any closer than the pages of this book, you will have still paid it a visit in your imagination. *Paranormal Confessions* is pure revelation, as Kristin has held nothing back, serving to vindicate or validate those who have made discoveries there of their own. "Haunted" seems an understatement as a description of this amazing place. The paranormal activity at Bellaire House is insidious and pervasive, well-documented, and off the spectrum. I know of what I speak. Having spent a decade of my life in a farmhouse alive with death, once opened, it is a door that never closes. Prepare yourself. It will be an enlightening journey—one you will never forget.

—Andrea Perron, author of *House of Darkness House of Light*

INTRODUCTION

Bellaire House

Sometimes it takes the fear of the unknown
to advance someone into the knowing and
understanding of what was and what is.

Kristin Lee

There are many haunted houses in the United States—
the Amityville house, the Winchester Mystery House,
the LaLaurie Mansion. Lizzie Borden's house, where
she infamously gave her father forty whacks with an
axe, now operates as a bed and breakfast. Even the
White House is said to be haunted; Winston Chur-
chill himself saw Lincoln's ghost coming out of the
bath! But for my money, the most haunted house
of all is a quiet-looking two-story house in Bellaire,
Ohio. And I should know—I lived there.

Bellaire House, located at the ordinary-sounding address of 1699 Belmont Street, was built by a man named Jacob Heatherington in 1847. It sits on top of both a ley line and an abandoned coal mine, close to sacred Shawnee burial caves and beneath a powerful planetary alignment. The house's location has thus always been a swirling cosmic whirlpool of immense spiritual power and paranormal activity. The tragic Heatherington family history—at least one family member died in the house—has only added to this mystique. When grief drove another family member to conduct countless séances and occult rituals there, eleven otherworldly portals were opened within the walls of the house. These portals can leech energy from the living, amplify demonic intent, and even cause dimensional slips in time. To this day, these portals remain open, beckoning forces both living and dead into the house.

I didn't know any of this when I first arrived on the steps of Bellaire House. My research into the house and the phenonmena behind its haunted happenings came much later, when I was desperate to make sense of the paranormal activity that I had experienced there.

Some people are born into haunted houses; I had mine thrust upon me. I found Bellaire House in 2005 when I was forced to relocate after the devastating loss of my own home in hurricanes Ivan and Frances. It was a foreclosure sale, so I could afford it, but no one ever told me that the property was haunted. During my time living there, I experienced all kinds of phenomena, from phantom footsteps in the attic, to ghostly figures that appeared and then disappeared in the blink of an eye, to objects that moved seemingly on their own. On one terrifying night, an invisible force even assaulted me and my beloved dog Bella.

The longer I spent in the house, the deeper it sank its claws into me. Eventually, after I was driven from my home by this activity, I tried to sell it—but to no avail. New owners and renters came and went, quickly chased out by the paranormal phenomena. No matter what I did, it seemed as if the house always came back to me. I began to ask myself this terrifying question: Did I find Bellaire House or did Bellaire House find me? Strange as it may seem, after all these years, I still own the house.

This book is about the spirits that dwell within Bellaire House. But it's also about the property's history and how I came to own one of the most notorious haunted houses in the world. Here, I present a collection of ghost stories, some of which are historical and some of which are deeply personal. Ghosts, demons, and spirit entities are all real, and haunted houses are far more than simple Hallowe'en attractions. If Bellaire House has taught me anything, it's that these forces are not to be trifled with.

At the end of each chapter, I have given a selection of helpful hints drawn from my own paranormal and spiritual experiences in hopes of providing paranormal investigators, both novice and experienced, with the knowledge and tools they need to facilitate better communication with the afterlife and to protect themselves from the negative energies that dwell in this and other haunted locations. The floor plans of the house, shown on the inside front and back covers, will help you better navigate the paranormal activities I describe there.

At Bellaire House, people have encountered child ghosts, malign entities, otherworldly occultists, the spirits of former slaves, incubi, and elementals. Guests and researchers alike have seen shadowy figures, full apparitions, and dark clouds of pure energy. Others have experienced all kinds of demonic assaults, both emotional and physical. Although the house's maelstrom of psychic energy makes it the perfect place to conduct séances or paranormal research retreats, visitors must beware: You never know what may come through. In describing the things I've witnessed personally and sharing my research, my goal has been to open the minds and hearts of readers to all matters paranormal. I hope that my experiences shed some light on phenomena that are seemingly inexplicable. So come inside. Bellaire House eagerly awaits you.

CHAPTER I

The Gray Man

Haunted houses are more common than you may think. Banish from your mind those images from famous horror movies, with walls dripping blood and ghosts rattling chains. Haunted houses can at first appear to be quiet places, just lovely normal dwellings. But they are all the more sinister for that. Do you sense a persistent unease within your home? Is there a room that's always freezing cold even in the middle of the warmest summer? Do you sometimes have an unshakeable feeling that something is watching you? Have you ever caught a glimpse of a shadowy figure out of the corner of your eye? Does your child's invisible friend seem more substantial and real than the run-of-the-mill imaginary playmate? If you answer "yes" to any of these questions, then congratulations—you may live in a haunted house!

I was taught at a very young age that there is life after death, but I never believed in haunted houses until I ended up owning one. I loved Caspar the Friendly Ghost as a child, but I was firmly told that he wasn't real, so I grew up assuming that all ghosts were like Caspar; they weren't real. For me, everything started at Bellaire House.

Owning a haunted house had never been on my bucket list. At the time I bought Bellaire House, all I wanted was a home—period. I had been living in Quincy, Ohio, when the quick succession of hurricanes Frances and Ivan destroyed my house. Layne and Nick, my two sons, our dog Bella, and I were deprived of every essential thing by the storms. I was still in graduate school, working full-time to make ends meet, and now we were homeless. Finally, someone from FEMA contacted me and told me that my family had received a grant that would enable us to relocate. So I began looking for a place to live—something modest and comfortable that would allow us to get settled and get back on our feet.

That was when I first stumbled across the address that would change my life: 1699 Belmont Street in Bellaire, Ohio. There were pictures of the house online—two stories, four bedrooms, two bathrooms, a dining room, living room, and foyer, lovely hard-wood floors, and real fireplaces. It even had a big yard for the boys and Bella to play in. I thought it was perfect! And it was a foreclosure, so I could afford it.

That evening after work, I met the realtor at the property. My first memory of the century-old house is of standing on the front porch and peeking through the bay windows at the hardwood floors. I remember that I liked the wooden hutch in the corner of the dining room. I even got lost in the house on that first visit because it was so big. I liked it immediately—the wood floors, the fireplaces, the windows, the brick floors in the kitchen and hallway. But it was when I walked upstairs to the attic that I fell in love.

The attic felt like a secret hiding place, a little nook away from it all. I felt as if I were walking in an enchanted garden and had found a secret glen off the beaten path. The ceiling's high portrait arches reminded me of a cathedral. Each wall had a small double window with wooden shutters set into a gable. If there was any sinister energy there, I certainly didn't notice it that day—at least, not that I remember. If I had experienced any negative feelings, I probably would have written them off or blamed them on the residual trauma of the past few months. I was finishing a Master's in forensic psychology at the time, so I knew very well how trauma can impact the mind. But none of that mattered in that moment as I stood in the attic. All I wanted was a new home and this house seemed perfect. I signed on the dotted line. Bellaire House was mine.

I was extremely happy with the house at first. It was the first time I had owned a home that I had purchased on my own, and I was pretty high on that rush you feel when you buy your first house. The first few days after we moved in, I honestly didn't notice anything paranormal—or even out of the ordinary, for that matter. Perhaps I felt so relieved to have found a nice place to live that I ignored what was happening around me. If a piece of furniture moved a few inches from where I had last seen it, or the floorboards creaked when no earthly feet were walking on them, I may have turned a blind eye. There were always other explanations. It was the wind. Old houses have creaks and quirks. Perhaps I'd simply forgotten where I put that missing item. After all, things don't just disappear on their own.

Looking back, I can see that I was desperate. I was utterly taken by the beauty and charm of my old-world home. I was numb after the hurricanes and the ensuing floods, and all I wanted was a safe place for my family to live. This house was supposed to be my sanctuary, my salvation, my American dream. Instead, it became my nightmare.

In hindsight, there's no denying the fact that I was experiencing an energy drain, although I didn't know what that meant at the time. I only knew that I felt wet-down and strangely soggy, as if I were carrying a heavy carpet full of flood water around with me everywhere. Living in the house made me feel separated from the outside world, as if I had drifted back in time. I blamed the flood. I blamed the trauma of losing my home. I blamed being suddenly uprooted. I blamed my huge workload. I blamed PTSD. Anything but the paranormal. How could I have known?

It started with footsteps. One day, I was puttering around the house when I suddenly heard someone walking upstairs in the attic. I froze, listening as the floor above me creaked beneath someone's weight. I was alone in the house. When the sound stopped, I let out a breath. The house is old, I told myself. The wooden floors are just settling. I put it out of my mind and went back to work in the kitchen. But then the sound started again. Creak. Creak. Creak. There *was* someone in the attic.

Hefe, the father of my son Layne, was living with us at the time. He'd taken a liking to the attic and had set up his tattoo parlor there. I told myself that he must be home after all, although I'd thought I was alone in the house. It was an easy mistake to make, after all, and I could hear the footsteps in the attic so clearly. What other explanation could there be? Imagine my surprise when Hefe later came through the front door. When I asked him if he'd been in the attic earlier, he said he hadn't. I *had* been alone in the house—just me and the footsteps upstairs. I felt as if there were something coming my way, the way people can sometimes feel a storm approaching. I felt it as a deep spiritual ache, a knowledge in my very bones. But the house was still beautiful and I didn't want to trust the feeling, so I pushed it away—until the house wouldn't let me ignore it any longer.

One night, I was sleeping in the living room. I had taken to sleeping down there on occasion because there was still a lot of work to be done on the house. Suddenly, I woke up, disoriented and unsure of what had roused me from sleep. I had the strangest sensation, as if something were somehow "off." The house was quiet; my family was still fast asleep. Everything seemed normal. Then I looked up and saw it. There was an apparition sitting next to me on the couch—a tall thin man with facial hair wearing a hat. He was gray in appearance, as if he'd stepped out of an old black-and-white movie. Most shocking of all, he was transparent.

I sat straight up and screamed.

"Who are you?" I demanded.

The Gray Man didn't answer—at least, not with words. Silently, he stood and walked into the foyer. Then he vanished in the blink of an eye, as if he had never been there at all. As I caught my breath, my heart hammering in my chest, I looked back down at the couch. There was a clear impression left in the cushion, a dip where the Gray Man had sat. It hadn't been a dream. In that moment, everything I thought I knew about my new house changed.

That was the first time I saw an entity in Bellaire House, but it wouldn't be the last. Things got progressively worse. I felt as if something were constantly trying to get my attention, working its way out of the ether to let me know it was there. Things went missing, only to turn up in places I could not possibly have put them. Objects moved all on their own. I became frightened of the second floor, where I felt most of the activity was taking place. I thought that maybe, if I stayed out of its space, whatever it was that was lurking up there would leave me alone. I moved all of Layne's toys and the television into the foyer. Our clothes ended up in the basement and a downstairs closet. "You can have the second floor," I thought. "I'll take the first floor and we can coexist—if not quite in peace, then at least in something like it." The entity, however, didn't agree. And what happened next terrified me to my core.

One night, I was lying in bed in what is now the Edwin Heatherington Room. Bella was in the room with me. It was a normal night—until it wasn't. An entity manifested as a black rain cloud that was full of static electricity. Instantly, the atmosphere in the room changed. I could feel a charge in the air; everything seemed to be pulsating with electricity. Before I could even register what I was seeing, I was forced backward and held down. It was utterly terrifying. Bella tried to protect me, barking and running around the room. She jumped on top of me, trying to defend me. This clearly disturbed the spirit, because one minute Bella was on top of me and the next she'd been thrown backward. Bella wasn't a large dog, but it still would have taken considerable force to throw her off. Panicked, I managed to scramble off the bed and Bella and I fled from the room.

Well, it was one thing to see apparitions, but it was another entirely to be attacked by one. I was scared beyond my limits. I knew I had to get out of that house before anything worse happened. I was afraid to be alone there and tried to have friends stay with me as often as possible. Everywhere I went in the house, I felt as if an unseen pair of eyes were staring at me, watching my every move. I continued to hear phantom footsteps, and sometimes an apparition appeared

Paranormal Confessions

out of nowhere right in front of me. I needed to get out of Bellaire House.

When I moved out in 2009, I swore to myself that I would never return. It seems strange to look back on that day and the feeling I had that I was leaving everything behind. But now I know that, in many ways, that was just the beginning. Months before I left, I had tacked a map up on the wall in my office and thrown a dart at it. I asked to be led spiritually to a greater good and my intention was to go wherever the dart landed, which turned out to be Massachusetts. We packed up and left. But, despite my every intention, it seemed that Bellaire House wasn't done with me yet. Before long, Bellaire's code enforcer called me and demanded that I return to take care of the property. I had to go back to Bellaire.

I tried every way I knew to get the house off my hands. It wasn't as if I were flush with cash, or wealthy enough to just let the property go. I was still a working mother in graduate school. So I decided to rent the house. But none of the renters ever stayed very long— the most determined only lasted a year. The house's hauntings were relentless. Tenants reported all kinds of paranormal activity. One had a chandelier fall, just missing his head, while another told me about experiencing a full-on physical assault. As the last set of renters pulled out of the driveway, I was left distraught, unsure what to do with my haunted house.

I drove back to the townhouse where I was living at the time, my head reeling, my heart full of fear that I might once again have to live in Bellaire House. I sat out on the porch and contemplated my options. I asked Apollo and Diana to show me a path to a greater good. As I sat there, I suddenly saw the Gray Man who had awakened me that night in the living room walking toward me. He looked the same—still transparent, still tall, still dressed in old-fashioned clothing. I had the strong sensation that he had come there specifically for me, that he knew where I had gone and had followed me. I was confused, wondering why he would follow me and not the departing tenants. After all, they had lived in the house much more recently than I. If he were going to follow anyone, wouldn't it have been them? But as he walked down the driveway, he turned and looked my way. He was definitely there for me.

Other people have seen the Gray Man. He's always transparent and always appears dressed in ragged clothes wearing either a farmer's hat or a trapper's cap. He has a long, aged face, and is commonly described as looking like Abraham Lincoln. Perhaps this is the reason why I and other investigators have had pennies thrown at our heads during our investigations into the house. Perhaps this is the Gray Man's way of telling us what he looks like. Not that I'll ever forget! The Gray Man was my first full apparition, and you never forget your first.

HELPFUL HINTS

Not all haunted houses exhibit paranormal activity on the level found at Bellaire House. There are many instances of activities that are not as hostile to living inhabitants, many examples of apparitions who are not so mercurial in mood. Sometimes it is even possible for people to live in these other haunted locations. But there are times when the energy may simply become overwhelming. If that is the case for you, there are things you can do to cleanse your home of negative energy and to keep malicious spirits at bay.

Wear hyacinth to guard against grief, nightmares, and crisis situations. It's known to help balance the soul and it can balance a house's soul as well. Hyacinth spreads a positive vibe across the psychic planes, invoking joy and strengthening spiritual communication with earthbound spirits. The fragrance is extremely uplifting. It can help manifest new love to heal a broken heart, and it also soothes grief during the transition of a loved one. Hyacinth eases the transition, helping the deceased to cross over into the afterlife more smoothly.

Infuse olive oil with hyacinth petals. You can soak an amulet in the oil and wear it for personal protection, or you can use the mixture as a cleansing floor wash. Washing the floors of your home with this wash will rid them of negative forces and replace negative with positive energy. Hyacinth incense helps to ward off all evil and can also be used to break a hex. Your home will feel brighter and the energy in it uplifted after you cleanse it with hyacinth, and you will find your space more peaceful. Hyacinth is a poisonous flower, however. Do not ingest it and keep it away from children and pets, especially cats.

CHAPTER 2

The First Family

It is impossible to discuss Bellaire House without talking about its original owners, the Heatheringtons. Strange as it may seem, several members of this family still reside in the house—or at least, their spirits do. Lyde Heatherington, who died in the house in 1947, haunts the premises, as does her mother, Eliza. Lyde's brother Edwin, a talented if unearthly psychic medium himself, is a frequent attendee at my séances. He has even appeared in my dreams.

The Heatherington family has a long history in Bellaire. John and Rebecca Heatherington immigrated to America from England in 1829. Their son Jacob followed them a year later. After some time, Jacob became a coal-mining tycoon but, despite his immense fortune, he remained a humble resident of the community. He worked beside his employees in the mines and even provided housing for them. When members of the community fell on hard times, he always helped them get back on their feet. Little by little, Jacob acquired an enormous holding of 677 acres of farming and mining lands, in addition to 110 acres of woodlands. He owned thirty houses, as well as a glass manufacturing concern, and railroad and steamboat stocks. In fact, Jacob became one of the largest taxpayers in Belmont County during his lifetime. His best friend, a mule named Jack, also became the stuff of legend when the famous nursery rhyme "The House That Jack Built" was written about him. Jack the mule lived to be an extraordinary forty years old and was buried in his own grave with a special marker.

Jacob built Bellaire House in 1847. His wife, Eliza Armstrong Heatherington, was a beautiful woman who had had a profound spiritual experience in her youth. One day, she saw a shooting star fall from the sky and decided that she would find it and keep it for her own. She went to the nearby Davis farm and knocked on the door to see if anyone else had seen the star fall. The door was opened by Mrs. Davis, a religious woman who believed that a falling star was a bad omen and that Eliza would be condemned to hellfire and brimstone if she followed it. She told Eliza to fall on her knees and pray, but Eliza didn't listen; she only wanted to find that star.

Eliza walked for miles, until she reached the banks of the Ohio River, where she was certain the star had fallen. She hid by the river until she was noticed by a man named Captain Fink, who introduced her to Jacob Heatherington. That falling star had led Eliza to the man who was to become her husband. Their marriage produced ten children, only eight of whom survived to adulthood.

When Jacob died in 1904 at the remarkable age of ninety, his middle son, Alexander, inherited the family coal-mining empire. Alexander is something of a tragic figure. He was committed to the Athens Asylum for the Insane in Athens, Ohio, late in life on the grounds that he had "lost the use of his manners" and was no longer of sound mind. His psychologist's notes give the cause of his mental state as "business troubles . . . [that] caused the trouble of domestic relations." Asylum paperwork also states that he had a "partial paralysis of one side of his body" as well as a stammer, and that he suffered from epilepsy.

Shortly after Alexander's commitment to the asylum, his daughter Lyde took over the Heatherington family's coal company. Lyde lived at Bellaire House, as did her younger brother, Edwin, after he was discharged from the military. Lyde died in 1947, reportedly in the dining room of the family home. Edwin, who had suffered the loss of another sister in his early youth, was consumed with grief upon Lyde's death. He became obsessed with the idea of contacting her in the afterlife through any means possible. He started studying the occult in an attempt to strengthen his own psychic abilities and make contact with his sister. He brought in occult experts and psychics from all over the country to help him in his cause. It's impossible for us to know now how many of these mediums and seers were authentic, but it's likely that some were charlatans who took advantage of Edwin's grief and his longing to connect with Lyde.

Many paranormal researchers who have investigated Bellaire House believe that Edwin unknowingly opened portals to the Other Side all over the house. According to our investigations, as many as eleven of these portals still exist in the house to this day. Despite attempts by paranormal investigators, psychic practitioners, and religious leaders to close them, the portals remain stubbornly open. One theory as to why is that Edwin was so depressed and distraught that he became oppressed and then possessed by the entities with whom he had made contact. As he dove deeper into the occult, his lack of proper training prevented him from closing the various portals he had opened. No one knows what Edwin experienced when he lived in the house alone. But from my own experiences there, I suspect his days were filled with terror.

To make matters worse, Edwin's remaining family members attempted to wrest ownership of the house from him. They ultimately succeeded in ousting him from the property, and it was at this point that the house left the Heatherington family's hands. Although he no longer owned the house, Edwin remained in Bellaire for the rest of his life. He died in 1962 at the age of seventy-five. He never married and had no children of his own; he was survived by a niece. And while he was removed from Bellaire House in life, his spirit returned to his ancestral home after his death.

I have personally communicated with Edwin many times over the years, and have had particular success contacting him using Steven Huff's portal, an audio/visual application that facilitates contact and communication with intelligent entities on the Other Side. During our communications, Edwin has told me that he wants me always to leave a chair open for him at the séance table, echoing the passion he had for séances during his lifetime. Because of this, our sessions always include what we refer to as "Edwin's seat." And there are consequences for anyone who dares to sit there.

When one group of women came to the house for a séance, I told them to leave a chair open for Edwin, as is our custom. They refused, instead putting a doll in his seat. Edwin quickly made his displeasure known. The chandelier in the foyer started blinking, as if he were telling us that this is his house and these are his rules! He wanted his seat back immediately. I walked into the Séance Room and asked the ladies again to leave a chair open for Edwin. When they refused a second time, a lightbulb in the chandelier exploded! The group finally removed the doll from the chair and let Edwin have his seat. After that, all was well, although Edwin held a grudge against the group and warned me to stay away from them. I was happy to oblige. After all, who comes to a haunted house to conduct a séance and then takes a chair away from one of the resident ghosts?

Over the years, I became curious to know what Edwin looked like during his lifetime. Despite my attempts, however, I never found any photographs of him. Finally, I asked Edwin's spirit to point me in the right direction. Shortly after that, I had a dream in which Edwin appeared. I could see that he had blue eyes and reddish hair. I tried not to think too much of it at the time. I knew that the mind is a funny thing and that it was possible that I had been thinking so much about Edwin during the day that my dreaming mind had simply manifested an image of him. I also refused to rule out the possibility that whatever had come to me in the dream wasn't actually Edwin, but rather a malign spirit posing as him as a way to get me to lower my guard. Still, I told a few people that I sensed that Edwin had blue eyes and reddish hair.

Months later, as I was going through documents I'd collected about the Heatherington family, I found Edwin's death certificate. I had seen this document before, but now saw that I had overlooked a key piece of information recorded there. His eyes were, in fact, blue. This discovery reassured me that there was a good chance it really was Edwin's spirit that had come to me as I slept. Perhaps he wanted to show me his physical self.

It's very important to us at Bellaire House that we honor and respect Edwin as the main psychic medium of the house. No one else is as successful as he is at communicating with us. Because he's a spirit, he has his own ways of contacting his fellow spirits who inhabit the house. Sometimes before investigations or events, I say: "Edwin, please go find Lyde. Please bring her to the table so we can ask her permission to have an event at the house." We have always received this permission—thanks, we think, to Edwin's intervention.

It's very important, when establishing communication with a spirit, to be polite and to speak your intent clearly. When I start my séance sessions, I always ask Edwin to join in. I begin by requesting that he say his name to confirm that he is there with us. In the past, I have had people challenge me, asking how I can know that the spirit communicating with me is truly Edwin and not an impostor. But when Edwin comes through and tells me that his name is Ed, I always feel reassured that it is, indeed, Edwin himself and not another entity impersonating him.

In our séances at Bellaire House, we use a protective circle and call upon deities of protection to banish any kind of negative energy or manipulation from hostile spirits. If, at any time, I feel as if it's not Edwin who is with us—for example, if I sense energy that is different from his familiar presence—we shut the circle down immediately. Sometimes I run additional tests to make sure that I am protecting myself and those around me, and I have told Edwin what some of these practices are so he knows how to respond in order to reassure me. Often, I ask him who cared for him as a child, both to confirm a specific answer that Edwin would know, and in order to confuse negative entities. The most common answer to that question is your mother. But we know that Edwin's mother, Elizabeth Anne Jones, did not take care of him when he was a child because she suffered from depression. It was actually Lyde who acted as a mother figure for Edwin when they were young. On two occasions when I have asked this question, an incorrect answer has alerted me to the fact that it wasn't Edwin speaking. I closed the circle immediately and did a thorough cleansing of the house.

When I first moved into Bellaire House, I visited a local optometrist to pick up new glasses—I had lost my old ones in the flood. As I waited for my glasses, I started talking with an old man sitting next to me. He was probably in his late eighties or early nineties. When I told him that I had just moved into the house, he said that he knew it very well and that "a seer" used to live there. Although I didn't know it at the time, I suspect now that he was referring to Edwin. When I returned home that day, I found that, for some reason, I was drawn to the dining room table, which stood right in front of the fireplace in roughly the spot where Lyde had died. I felt a cold chill go through me. Though there was no one else in the room with me, I didn't feel alone; I felt as if I were being watched. Today, I understand that this was Edwin's way of showing me he was there. He was attempting to guide me, letting me know that the dining room, which we now call the Séance Room, was the epicenter of a larger spiritual presence in the house.

Sometimes the energy inside Bellaire House can get out of hand. There are a lot of different energies that circulate there, and it can be physiologically draining, not only to myself, but also to guests and other paranormal researchers. I always call upon Yemaya and Obatala, my spiritual parents, and San Miguel (Archangel Michael), then I immediately call upon Edwin, Lyde, Eliza, and Jacob as the spirits of the house to surround us so we can fight off any negative energy together. We have to work *with* spirit to battle negative entities. It's the only way we can wear them down.

One of the most disturbing explanations I've heard for the haunted history of Bellaire House is that a malign force uses Edwin to speak for all of the spirits in the house. Another claims that Edwin is under the command of a hostile force. One thing we do know about the spirits in the house is that they seem to operate in a sort of hierarchy, with the attic's entity at the top. Some people have even theorized that this entity is actually Lyde in disguise and that it is she who rules the house. Given my personal experiences with the spirits of both Lyde and Edwin, however, I don't put much stock in this, because the attic entity sometimes seems to "go away." There are periods when its negative energy becomes dormant—although, in the end, it always comes back. To this day, I and other paranormal researchers remain unsure how to banish it permanently from the house. One thing I know for certain, however: Conjuring pulls you into a certain realm of energy. Perhaps this is how Edwin and Lyde became trapped in their afterlife inside Bellaire House.

HELPFUL HINTS

When holding a séance, circle your table or investigation space with kosher salt. Add rue, apple seeds, and sunflower seeds or sunflower petals to create a circle of charged positive energy. You can also wear a pair of shiny silver sewing scissors on a chain around your neck to prevent any type of psychic or paranormal attack. The scissors "cut away" any negative energy that may attempt to creep up on you. Or you can wear a necklace with a small mirror suspended from it instead of sewing scissors. I have a necklace with a silver mirror that I often wear. Both the silver and the mirror are reflective surfaces; when an entity catches sight of its reflection in the silver or the mirror, it turns away. This is an excellent way to protect yourself from negative entities and energies during a séance.

When opening a séance, it is always best to introduce yourself first. I start by saying: "Hello, I am Kristin Lee. I come in peace; I come with love. I would like to talk to you and learn about your world." You can use this format for your own séances—just replace my name with your own. It's also best for other participants to hold hands and speak their names, each adding: "I come with love and in peace to communicate with and learn about you."

CHAPTER 3

A Valentine's Day Investigation

As a special Valentine's Day event, our afterlife research team hosted a paranormal investigation for couples. Unlike some of our events, this one was open to the general public. The goal was for the guests to enjoy an evening collecting paranormal data with their loved ones before spending the night in the house. When guests first arrived, they checked into their rooms, then met us downstairs for dinner. After dinner, we planned to conduct a séance in the parlor.

We had quite the team that night. Jon Campbell and Allison Welly, a student of metaphysics who has helped me operate Bellaire House for more than five years, set up the DVR system, while psychic medium Susan Curtis, paranormal investigator Jim Backus, and my personal friend Tina Arnold arrived before our guests to help Layne and me prepare for the night. Four couples, some romantic pairs and some close friends, participated in the event. As always, it was interesting to watch the dynamics among our guests. Some were seasoned paranormal investigators; others were first-time visitors to a truly haunted location.

The first to arrive were two ladies who were going to stay in the study, the room that leads up to the attic that used to be my office. Tina showed them to their room as Greg and Bonnie, our second pair of guests, arrived. The house's effect on Greg was immediately apparent. He didn't greet anyone as he came into the parlor; he was flustered and red in the face. I could tell that he was overwhelmed by the house's energy and that he needed a distraction. When I noticed that Bonnie wore an Eagles "Hotel California" T-shirt, I said: "Great band! Did you check out their concert last night? Tickets were outrageous!"

My attempt to distract Greg didn't work. He began to walk around the parlor, clutching a crystal pendant in one hand and raising the other in an attempt to connect with the house's energies. As he reached the foyer, he said: "I feel a heart attack . . . I feel a child . . . I see and hear an old woman talking. Is there someone upstairs?"

Concerned, I put my hand on Greg's arm and told him that perhaps he should try to be less open right at the start. Knowing that he would soon have a headache, I told Jim and Susan that, if he began to feel ill, they should have him step outside to ground himself. In all my time at Bellaire House, I have never seen anyone be so immediately open to its energy as Greg was. There was not much I could do to help but warn him; I knew from experience that he was going to be a target during the séance that night and that the team would have to keep a watchful eye on him to ensure both his safety and that of the other guests.

When guests arrive at Bellaire House, I often get extra-sensory feelings about them. Nine times out of ten, these initial impressions are confirmed during the séance. I was sure that this would happen again as our the third couple arrived. Krista and Maria were two local girls in their early twenties who were unseasoned paranormal investigators. They both had great energy; they were full of life and both had a very positive vibe. I immediately sensed that Krista was broken-hearted over the loss of a parental figure and that she wore a smile in order to hide her grief. I felt that she had come to connect with a deceased loved one and that she desperately desired confirmation that there is an afterlife. It felt to me as if Maria had lost a different kind of love, as if she had recently—and perhaps unwillingly—ended a romantic relationship.

Krista and Maria were scheduled to spend the night in the Altar Room. As I showed them to the room, I told them a little bit about its history. It had, at one time, been my bedroom when I still lived at Bellaire House. When the house was at the peak of its paranormal activity, I used that room to protect my family and myself by petitioning and casting protection circles there. I told the girls that I personally felt it was the safest room in the house, but that many other investigators had collected paranormal data there.

Once the girls were settled in, I told them to treat the house as if it were their own home and asked them to meet me in the Séance Room in about an hour. As I left the room, I heard Allison, Bonnie, and Greg talking in Emily's room, where Greg and Bonnie were scheduled to spend the night. This room is right by the stairs, so I stopped by to see what was going on. I found Greg slowly turning in circles. He seemed perplexed, as if he wanted to speak, but the words just wouldn't come out. I asked him what he was feeling and he kept pointing to a wall that I knew contained one of the house's many portals. This showed me that what he was experiencing was valid, but I kept this information to myself for the time being. I wanted to see if he downloaded anything more during the séance. ("Download" is the term I use for the way spirits read energy off a person, in the same way that files can be downloaded from a computer.)

I walked downstairs to greet the final guests, a married couple from the Pittsburgh area. Unlike my reaction to Krista and Maria, I found that I was unable to read their energy. This typically happens when someone has erected a psychic shield of protection. This couple didn't introduce themselves—although I knew from the reservation that the husband's name was Brandon—and they kept to themselves. I couldn't tell if their guarded attitude resulted from meeting new people or from the atmosphere of the house. Brandon and his wife were shown to the Edwin Heatherington Room to get settled before the séance.

I had ordered pizza and sandwiches so everyone could get comfortable and enjoy a meal before we really got started. As the guests mingled, Jim Backus and I went out to the back of the house to sit on the porch. It was nice to have a moment to ourselves to relax before the séance. As we discussed how we were going to proceed that night, I noticed that Jim kept staring into the woods behind the house. Finally, I said: "Jimmy, what's up? You seem spaced out!"

Jim shook his head and smiled at me, then said: "There's something human-sized rustling in the woods. I feel as if we're being watched." I told him that it was probably a coyote. He paused for a moment and then said: "It's not an animal. I think it's human or something attached to the land, like a Native American or a French soldier. Something is watching us."

Jim had been my teammate for more than four years and had twenty-five years of investigations under his belt, yet I had never seen him like this or heard him express the belief that something was watching us. As it was almost time for the séance to begin, I told him we should go back inside and that we would use the front of the house instead of the back to take breaks, just in case.

As Jim and I re-entered the house, I could feel that the energy inside was starting to amplify itself a hundred times over. Privately, I thought that Greg was the cause of this. In his desire to be in touch with the house's energy, he was opening himself up to the spirits and entities inside the house. I was concerned that this openness would make him a target during the séance, but I couldn't worry too much about him, as I had to watch out for the safety of all the guests. When everyone was gathered in the room, I opened the séance. I stood up with my hands out to my sides and my feet apart, making my body a pentacle. I called upon San Miguel and invoked Yemaya and Obatala to protect me and those with me. I asked the spirits of Bellaire House and my ancestors to join me and to raise the energy so high that we would shine like a beacon, our light attracting all those with whom we wished to communicate.

With our lines of spiritual communication open, I began to walk around the table as I raised the energy and vibrations in the room. One by one, the guests introduced themselves and made their intentions known to the spirits by saying: "I come with love and in peace to communicate with and learn about you."

We asked: "Can you see us?"

"Perfectly," said the spirits. "We are guiding you."

We asked: "What is your name?"

"Elizabeth," one spirit responded. Then we heard the word "Vampire."

Greg said: "Touch me."

"I don't think you want to do that," came the response. Then a spirit said: "Go to the spot. Do you feel that? Very awesome. Triple gods." This spirit continued to communicate with us, saying: "The world is a bit off. Overtime. It's in the books. It's so peaceful . . . daughter." This message was for Krista from her departed father, letting her know that it was peaceful where he was in the afterlife.

"The final thing you want to do," a spirit said. "Energy, you know she owns it."

At this point, the spirits began talking among themselves. We had set up a variety of paranormal equipment for the séance, including a Boo Buddy, an interactive electronic device that is shaped like a teddy bear, and a spirit, or ghost, box, a piece of equipment that uses radio frequency sweeps to generate white noise that is believed to give entities the energy they need to be heard. At one point, we clearly heard the spirits say: "Master-level spirits . . . they are staying here tonight."

"You are a little tiny bit off," another spirit said. At this point, I knew that Greg was being downloaded. Then a female spirit said: "Allow me to help you, Greg . . . by the window. I promise."

Greg broke the séance circle when he heard a spirit say: "Go to the window behind you, look right." He went to the right side of the window and put his hand above his head to feel the energy. He had no idea that he was standing directly on a ley line. The spirit said: "I'm downloading you . . . healing energy." In response, Greg took off his coat, then ripped off his protective amulets and threw them down on the table. Immediately concerned, I told him: "You may not want to do that."

"I'm fine. I'll be okay," he replied. "I want to know and feel this energy."

I could see that I wasn't going to be able to reach Greg no matter what I said to him. I knew that he was in a trance and that a malicious entity had overtaken him. As he began to remove his shirt, Eliza Heatherington, one of the spirits of the house, came through and clearly said: "Shut it down."

I immediately directed Jon to shut down the session and I turned the lights back on. Every person in the room was on the edge of his or her seat, except for Greg. He was swaying back and forth. I walked over to him and put my hand on his shoulder.

"Greg, you've got to come back to us," I said, gently shaking him a bit until he snapped out of the trance.

"That was amazing," Greg said when he was aware of his surroundings again. He told me that he was fully charged and that he felt better than he ever had. I was disappointed in his reaction because of the potential harm he could have suffered. I knew that I would not be physically able to help him if he collapsed or if the entity overtook him and then passed through him to reach other guests or my team.

After a break, I asked everyone to gather in the parlor so we could regroup our energy and ground ourselves. I explained the amount of energy we had channeled and asked if everyone wanted to go back into a séance session. They all agreed that they wanted to continue. I explained to Greg that, no matter what happened, he had to remain in the circle. Jon started the Steven Huff portal and used Keith Weldon's

Spiritus, a mobile app used for spirit communication. We placed radiating electromagnetism pods (REM pods) in each corner of the room. These devices radiate their own electromagnetic fields, making them more powerful and more sensitive than traditional electromagnetic flux meters that can only detect electromagnetic fields produced by flowing currents of electricity. This is thought to allow spirits to communicate more easily. The pods are small circular devices with five colored LED lights on top that the spirits can light up to make their presence known. We also placed some twist mag flashlights alongside the Boo Buddy.

"If you can see us," Jim said as we started the séance, "please light up the REM pod." The pod lit up in confirmation that there was a spirit in the room who wished to communicate. Susan Curtis spoke next: "If you can see us, please light up the REM pod by the fireplace." Within seconds, the second pod lit up. When Susan asked the spirit to turn the light off, the pod's light went out.

Krista then asked if she could try to communicate with her deceased father. She broke the circle to hold a copper wire on the portal in order to make a better connection of personal energy with him.

"Dad, can you hear me?" Krista said. "It's me, Krista." She waited a few moments for a verbal response, but none came. I directed her to speak about treasured memories she shared with her father in order to strengthen the connection. As she began to speak about personal moments, a voice came through and said: "Hi." After a few moments, the voice said: "Daughter." Krista told her father that she missed him. His spirit indicated that he was at peace and watching over her from the afterlife. As Krista came back to the circle, the voice again said: "Daughter."

Then Brandon asked if he could try to communicate with his own father. He walked over to the Huff portal and placed his hands on it to put out his personal energy. As he started asking questions, the atmosphere in the room shifted very suddenly. It felt as if a swirl of energy were coming up through the floor, and it was easy to see that it began to affect everyone. Some of the guests began to fidget in their seats. I tried my best to monitor them, but I quickly became lightheaded. The temperature dropped so much that a few of the participants commented on it, saying that the room was getting colder or that they felt cold. The chill was the result of the spirit taking energy from the room and using it to communicate with us.

Suddenly, I felt the presence of a stronger entity enter the room. As it passed through me, Layne leaned over and whispered: "Something just came in here. It feels like the entity in the attic."

I began to feel dizzy. I tried to push through the feeling as I told Jim to take Layne outside immediately. Once Layne was safely outside, I told Susan to prepare for an energy overload. I leaned forward and put my head in my hands. I had started to lose my vision when I heard Allison, who was on the couch in the living room, state that something had grabbed her legs and pulled off her shoe. A strange feeling came over me, and I called out to her: "Do you feel as if you are in Iraq?" I tried to describe what I was experiencing. "I feel as if I'm killing people in a war." Overcome by the energy, I made a decision and told Susan that I needed to step out.

I went outside to get some fresh air and shake off the energy for a few minutes, then went to the living room to lie down. As I lay there, I could hear Brandon talking to an entity in the parlor and other guests reacting to the responses he was getting. When Susan came to check on me, she told me that Brandon had served on the front lines in the Middle East. She was just about to tell me how many people he'd killed when I cut her off. "Forty people," I said. And just as I spoke, I heard the spirit box echo me: "Forty people."

Brandon continued his communication for a little while longer, but I had to refrain from tuning in to his energy or focusing on the séance. I had to leave it to Jon and Jim to shut down the session and lead the group in their investigation of the house. Unfortunately, given how drained the séance had left me, I wasn't able to join them, although I tried to last as long as I could so I could say goodnight to everyone before they turned in. I was thankful that I had some great teammates to help me with the event that night.

Later, Jon reported that the guests did have other paranormal experiences during their investigation of the house. He also told me that, when he rewound the DVR recording of that night, he identified something in the living room with Allison, but that he was later able to rule out that it was the malicious entity from the attic. We remain unable to explain exactly what pulled off Allison's shoe, and we are still unsure what entity came through during the séance and overtook Greg.

Brandon did share with Jon that he had made a connection with his platoon-mates who had been killed in battle. He also thought that he may have communicated with some of the people he had killed. It took a lot for him to open up to that kind of energy and to relive those horrific moments of his life. I believe the attic entity tried to wear me down that night in order to attack Brandon. Unfortunately, I never had the chance to tell him how much I appreciated his military service. I would never have imagined that the night would be so intense and so full of such varied spiritual communication. But I do know that the energy of Bellaire House shifts constantly. You can never truly predict what will happen inside it. The house has its own heartbeat and many personalities. It is a living melting pot of spirits and metaphysical energies.

HELPFUL HINTS

If you want to participate in a séance in a haunted house, always seek out a practitioner who is well-schooled in the paranormal. It is safest never to attempt a séance inside your own home simply for fun. It is also a best practice always to wear a protection pouch, or mojo bag, during a séance. You can make one by wrapping iron nails first in a red cloth and then in a silver cloth. If you have or can find wolf hair, put it inside the pouch along with the nails to help protect you from negative energy. When you submit yourself to paranormal energies, like those present in Bellaire House, you will likely feel some type of physical effect. The protection pouch won't guard you completely, but it will keep you safer.

CHAPTER 4

Emily Davis

One of the most notable and infamous inhabitants of Bellaire House is Emily Davis—a spirit who manifests as a young child, a little girl in a white dress. Most people who have seen her report that she has sandy-blonde hair, although some have described her hair as dark. The term "child spirit" can be misleading, however. A child spirit takes on the appearance or form of a child, but is not necessarily the spirit of a once-living child.

I have seen Emily myself. Once, I decided to sit on the roof so I could watch a Harvest Moon rise over the Ohio River while I played my guitar. To get the best view, I had to sit sideways on the roof, so I was also able to see back into my office through the window. As I sat there playing my guitar, I saw the office door open out of the corner of my eye. I figured that my husband, Daniel, had come home and I called out to him. He didn't answer. By that point, I was well aware that the house was haunted, so I just figured that the spirits were up to their usual tricks. A few moments later, however, I saw the apparition of a little girl in a white dress walk into the office and go upstairs to the attic. I felt a chill go down my spine and decided it was time to go back inside. This is just one of the experiences I have had with Emily.

The first time I heard Emily's voice was in 2009, right as I was about to pack up and leave Bellaire House in an attempt to restart my life. I was in the attic with Danny Hwang and Mike McCallister, two paranormal researchers who were there to train me, and we were attempting to communicate with the spirits of the house using an old Shack Hack, a radio device that continuously scans AM and FM frequencies to create white noise. Emily came through and said: "Hi, Kristin." It was the first time I ever had a spirit communicate with me through electronic equipment, and I was completely shocked to hear her use my name. I could hardly believe it. It briefly crossed my mind that someone might be playing a practical joke on me, but I didn't think so. When I asked the spirit her name, she responded: "Emily." After a few moments pause, she added: "Davis."

The spirit sounded like a child, so I asked what her favorite game was and she told me it was tag. I was nervous, because I knew that spirits can take on the voices or forms of children as a ruse. It's ingrained in our human nature to trust in the innocence of children, and some entities take advantage of that trust. So I backed up my energy; I wasn't going to fall for any tricks.

When making contact with a spirit, I always think in terms of the "where" (the haunted location), the "when" (the time in history when the location was most active), and the "who" (the spirit in question). My research had shown me that the majority of Bellaire residents from 1800–2009 were Christians, so I used trigger words that Emily would recognize if she were, in fact, the spirit of a child who had once lived in the town.

"Emily," I said, "I am here to help you go to heaven," knowing that the word "heaven" would likely evoke a strong reaction either way. If this really was the spirit of a child, she would react positively to the word; if she was not an earthly entity, she would react negatively to it. Emily repeated the word "heaven" back to me, which seemed to confirm that she was an earthly spirit.

After this session, Danny, Mike, and I took a break to get some dinner. As I was pulling out of the driveway at the back of the house, Mike walked up to my car and began pounding on the window and pointing to the attic. The entire attic was lit up in purple and blue lights! I was absolutely confounded. I knew I had turned off all the lights before we left. I always did that as a safety precaution—the old roof leaked and I didn't want to risk an electrical fire. There was no way the lights could have turned back on without some kind of interference. We managed to catch all of this on film and, as a result, we were invited to appear on the television show *My Ghost Story*. Later, we learned that Emily Davis especially likes to play with what she calls the "beautiful lights" of the K2 meter, a portable device that detects spirit activity and alerts investagtors to high electromagnetic-field radiation.

In later sessions, we discovered that Emily was under the control of the attic's evil entity, who acts like the ringleader of the Bellaire House spirits. If the house were a high school, it would be the meanest kid in school. It forces the other entities within the house to do its bidding, including Emily, who has been under its power for so long that she has conformed to its evil demands. She acts as an informer for this entity, collecting any information that people give her and whispering it in its ear. This is just one of the reasons why we tell those who visit the house not to talk about their families, their pets, or their personal lives. Bellaire House will take that information and twist it and use it against you, leaving you vulnerable to paranormal attack.

The Emily Davis entity can be very deceptive. Despite appearances, Emily isn't a child—she is what we call an "unclassified entity." She can shapeshift and even manifest as multiple entities simultaneously. She drains energy, especially during confrontations, and engages in multiple levels of manipulation at once, which makes attempts to research her exceedingly difficult. I encountered this aspect of Emily many times in 2016 as I delved deeper into my paranormal research. The first few times, I found that I was unable to retain my focus because of the way she engaged with me. I was challenged, and I risked succombing to my deepest fears. Emily didn't like that I refused to back down, but I had questions that needed to be answered. One thing I wanted to know was whether the story of Emily trying to lure a group of children onto the house's roof were true.

When I was still living at Bellaire House, some neighborhood kids came over to play video games with my son. You can only imagine my shock and horror when I saw them climbing out onto the roof through a bedroom window. I quickly nipped that plan in the bud. After I closed and locked the window, I asked them what had ever given them the idea to climb out onto the roof. They told me that a little girl in a white dress had told them to go onto the roof and play. After I sent the children home, I confronted Emily to find out if this story were true. The entity didn't like it when I refused to abandon my line of questioning. When challenged, Emily behaves like a bratty child who isn't getting her own way, or like a slippery snake slithering deeper into the underworld energies. In a spiritual battle, she becomes sinister, cold, and dead, and shows no mercy.

Unlike typical malign entities, Emily feeds on sadness rather than fear in order to stay charged. I've personally found that the energy level of anyone engaging with her is very low. To the inexperienced, this drop in energy may initially feel almost mellow, with a slight sting of electricity. At first, it may feel as if she is charging you physically. But what's actually happening is that she is using you as an energy source.

Researching Emily has proven to be something of a challenge. We know that she was a descendant of Jacob Davis, who first founded the settlement that would become Bellaire in 1802. Other spirit residents of Bellaire House have told us that she drowned when she was a child, and we have managed to document that a child named Emily Davis did, in fact, drown in the Ohio River. I also learned that Emily used to play at Bellaire House with the Heatherington children. In fact, during my research, I discovered that there are actually two different spirits within the house that go by the name Emily Davis. The second Emily isn't a child spirit, however; she is older. As with many spirits of the house, it has been difficult to find information about who this older Emily was when she was alive. We think she may have been a friend of Jacob Heatherington during her lifetime.

It doesn't surprise me that there are two different spirits named Emily connected with Bellaire House. One fascinating aspect of the house is that it attracts people, both living and dead, with similar names. Once, two men with the same first and last name showed up at the house at the exact same time. They didn't know each other, but, because of the house, they began working together. One explanation behind this phenomenon is that a dimensional slip in time draws in people from the past, the present, and the future. Think of it as a spiritual black hole whose force attracts those with specific names. Sometimes the entities that reside in the house use this to trick and confuse investigators, making them question exactly with whom they're communicating.

Today, the child-spirit Emily has her own room in the house—the first room on the left as you walk up the stairs to the second floor. The large and spacious room contains three big windows and a beautiful light-blue marble-and-wood fireplace. There are two portals in the left-hand corner of the room. When I first lived in the house, it was Layne's bedroom. Emily told us during a data collection that she wanted that room. She is a very frequent communicator and especially likes to talk during EVP (electronic voice phenonmena) sessions and on the ghost box. For as long as I've known of her existence, Emily has always greeted me with the words: "Hi, Kristin." One thing I don't understand about her, however, is why she continues to pose as a child with me. If she's a malicious entity, she possesses intelligence and should know by now that I don't believe she is truly a harmless child spirit.

It's very common for those who come to investigate Bellaire House to make contact with Emily. Many investigators treat her in much the same way they would a real living child and believe she is harmless. One investigator in particular became very attached to her. He says that she comforted him when he told her he was ill. He believes that she followed him home and has been with him there for many years. I watched a Facebook Live feed that showed him and his team communicating with a spirit that seemed to be Emily. If it truly was, this means that Emily can travel outside of Bellaire House and attach herself to other people.

Our groundskeeper, Goat, frequently greeted people arriving at Bellaire House for weekend investigations. He had done this for years with few issues. One day in 2017, he told me that, as he waited for one of the teams to arrive, he lay down on the couch to rest his eyes. As he lay there, he felt a cold chill enter his body. He tried to cover himself up to chase away the chill, but it stubbornly remained. Then a nearby REM pod went off, and he sat up and opened his eyes.

"Emily, is that you?" he asked. The pod went off again, confirming to him that it was, indeed, Emily. He looked into the Séance Room and saw that, despite the fact that he was alone in the house, a Saint Michael candle had been lit. He called me in a panic and asked me to come and sit with him while he waited for the visiting team. When I arrived, he told me that he was sure that Emily had caused the activity, but that he didn't understand why she was trying to scare him. A few weeks later, he started experiencing paranormal activity in his own home. Doors slammed shut on their own; he heard footsteps running in the attic; in the middle of the night, his blankets were pulled off him.

It was around this time that Daniel and I noticed a sudden change in Goat's personality; he became irritable and mean. In the ten years I had known him, I had never heard him use profanity, but suddenly, it became a frequent occurrence. Daniel, who worked with him at a nearby casino, told me that he had become mean to the guests and his coworkers as well. I began to call Goat nightly to check in. One night, he was incredibly irate, cursing and saying foul things in a way that was completely unlike him. When I called him at home to ask what was going on, he told me that, every time he tried to open a can of soup, the electric can opener blew. I decided to see what was going on, so I called a few other investigators to help me determine if Emily had attached herself to him. We decided we would run two investigations at once. I would try to connect with Emily at Goat's house, while my team would simultaneously attempt to determine whether Emily had somehow left Bellaire House.

When I started the session at Goat's house, I asked: "Who is here with us?" Sure enough, Emily came through and said: "Emily."

"Did you come home with me, Emily?" Goat asked. He didn't get an immediate response. When the team at Bellaire House checked in, they reported that their data collection had initially detected minimal activity.

Around 11 p.m., I asked: "Emily, did you leave Bellaire House and follow Goat home?"

"Hi, Kristin," Emily said, as she usually does when communicating with me. "Yes, he is my friend."

Goat asked: "Emily, are you trying to scare me?" The response was a very emphatic: "No!" Then he asked: "Did you pull the covers off me?"

"Yes," Emily replied. "I am cold."

Goat told Emily to go back home and that she wasn't allowed to live with him. He said that her home was Bellaire House, not his house. Her response was violent. She said: "F*** you, Goat!" This happened at around 11:45 p.m. Then the Bellaire House team called me to report that the doors upstairs had slammed and that the energy had shifted suddenly inside the house, indicating that Emily had returned home.

This is far from the only time that Emily became violent. I once coordinated with a local casino that was holding a major paranormal convention to provide accommodations for participants. A very dear friend of mine named Carrie oversaw the twelve guests who spent the weekend at Bellaire House. Every bedroom was full. Carrie woke up early to cook breakfast for everyone. As she was frying bacon in the kitchen, Mike, Carrie's teammate, smelled the bacon and went into the kitchen to help. To his horror, he found Carrie standing beside the stove with a pan full of hot bacon grease in her hand. She was pouring the grease onto her leg. He lunged and grabbed the pan. Carrie's leg was badly burned, and he described her as being in a trance.

"Carrie, Carrie, come back," Mike shouted, shaking her by the shoulders. "Where the hell are you?" He grabbed a bottle of water and splashed it on her face, with no effect. She was white as a sheet and remained utterly unresponsive. When I arrived at the house minutes later, I found Carrie stretched out on the couch with Mike caring for her. Luckily, one of the guests was a nurse; she told us that Carrie had second-degree burns. After some time, Carrie came back to us, but appeared not to remember anything that had happened. She actually tried to get up and finish cooking, and refused to go to the ER for treatment despite our entreaties. In my research into this disturbing event, I discovered that one of the more threatening facets of Emily's personality had put Carrie into a trance and caused her to burn her leg, although we don't know the reason behind this extremely malicious attack.

In 2019, when I found I needed a break from both Bellaire House and my career as a psychic advisor, I enrolled in a nail-technology program for a fun change of pace. I made friends quickly because I was interesting and spooky, not because I was a great nail tech. After all, I had been on television, which made me a big fish in a small pond. One day, when some of the girls and I were eating lunch in the basement of a creepy old building, the talk turned to ghost stories. One of the girls was named Emily, so the conversation naturally turned to Emily Davis. Suddenly, the lights began to flicker and the napkins flew off our lunch table, although it was simply not possible for a natural draft to have moved them. I pulled out my phone and opened an app called iOvilus that produces speech based on changes to sensors on the phone in order to facilitate spirit communication. As soon as I opened the app, I heard: "Bellaire . . . Emily!"

Immediately, all of the girls freaked out. In spite of, or perhaps because of, the shock, they were intrigued, and all of them wanted to visit Bellaire House. One of my classmates even brought a haunted doll to the house so she could give it to Emily.

HELPFUL HINTS

Many cultures believe that giving spirits or entities gifts may appease them, and that tradition continues today at Bellaire House with Emily Davis. Over the years, Emily has frequently requested that people send her toys, claiming that all of her old toys are now long gone. Now, many investigators bring her gifts when they visit the house. Others have mailed her teddy bears, dolls, and all sorts of other playthings. If you ever visit the house, feel free to bring along a present for Emily—just take care not to invite her home with you.

CHAPTER 5

Lockdown

One of the options we offer paranormal investigators at Bellaire House is a full lockdown. During a lockdown, an investigation team enters the house and remains there for a set amount of time—anywhere from one night to several days—in order to gather paranormal data. During a lockdown, team members are subjected to the full force of the house's energy. In a haunted location as mercurial and powerful as Bellaire House, lockdown investigations can be dangerous, so we have specific rules for investigative teams, in addition to our rules for regular guests. For instance, we insist that no one be in the house alone, and that everyone enter the house in pairs. No one is allowed inside until residual energies have been given a few days to dissipate, and researchers are encouraged to break off their investigations if they start to experience paranormal activity that is affecting their day-to-day lives. Items that may trigger these paranormal activities, like haunted objects or ashes of the deceased, are strictly banned. These rules are all enforced for the protection of the teams.

One memorable lockdown involved a paranormal team from Jamestown, New York, who had come to film a documentary. I was held up by car trouble and was unable to greet them on the first day, so Kat Lang, who was to play an important role in the story of Bellaire House, went in my stead. My car's battery had just been jumped when I received a phone call from Kat saying that I needed to get down to the house immediately. Something, she told me, had whipped her. She needed my help.

I pulled into the driveway of Bellaire House around 10 p.m. I called Kat from my car and asked her to give me the rundown on what had happened one more time so that I could properly prepare myself to handle whatever situation awaited me inside the house. She told me that she and the visiting team had been in the basement when, suddenly, she heard a sound like the cracking of a whip. Then she felt something strike her leg. The other investigators reportedly felt a gust of air pass over their faces, as if someone had quickly lifted a whip back up. I had never before, in all the time I had known Kat, heard her sound so shaken.

"I'm telling you," Kat insisted, "the demon is posing as Emily tonight. All of you are in danger." Alarmed, I asked her just how strong she thought the malicious energy was. She told me that it was strong enough that she felt she had to leave, and that fact alone should have told me everything I needed to know. "I was physically hurt," she said, "and if this thing hurt me, then I'm very worried about all of you!"

I first met Kat in the company of Bishop James Long, about whom you'll hear more in chapter 9. At the time, she gave me a gift—a pink crucifix that hangs on the rearview mirror of my car. As I sat in the car talking to Kat, the crucifix slowly started to tilt sideways. It swayed like a pendulum, back and forth, and I watched in horror as it turned itself upside down. When I showed Kat a phone video of the cross, she urged me to go home, telling me that the investigating team, not I, had wanted this experience. Panicked, I told her I at least had to fill the team in on the rules of investigation and let them know that they could contact me if they needed anything, but she kept begging me to go home. Finally, I relented. But when I tried to start my car, the engine would not turn over. I had no choice; the car wouldn't start, and I had to go into the house.

Kat was furious. "I'm warning you," she said, "Someone on this team is going to get hurt tonight. You know the rules—when the house is bad, we walk away and let it have its fit. You made the rule, so why are you breaking it?"

Looking back on that night, it's clear to me that the house's energy was overtaking both Kat and myself. I truly feel that the house was doing its level best to turn us against each other. I believe this is why, just as I decided to go home, the house stalled my car. And it wasn't finished with me, either. The next thing I knew, my phone started to emit a high-pitched noise, like a siren, and I lost my connection with Kat. There I was, sitting all alone in the driveway of a haunted house in the middle of the night with a dead cell phone and an engine that wouldn't start. All the while, the upside-down crucifix attached to my rearview mirror swung back and forth as if to taunt me.

By this time, I knew that I really didn't want to go inside Bellaire House that night. I waited a little longer, repeatedly trying to start my car, but no matter what I did, the engine refused to turn over. I felt myself getting more and more frustrated with every failed attempt, but I forced myself to stay calm. I knew that the entity fed off fear, anger, and sadness, and I wasn't about to become a one-woman buffet for it. I put my head down on the steering wheel and started to visualize calming, positive images like the ocean, and I called on Jesus Christ to walk into the house with me. All of a sudden, there was a loud bang on my window. I jolted up with a scream, startled out of my skin. On the other side of the window stood Austin, a neighborhood boy.

"I'm sorry. I didn't mean to scare you," he said. "I just wanted to see if Layne was with you so we could get together tonight." Relieved to see another living face, I told him that Layne wasn't with me that night, but that they could hang out tomorrow. Austin opened the car door for me and told me he would see me safely inside, because I was "old and a chicken." I told him to go home and that I'd see him tomorrow. He continued to stand by the car to make sure that I got inside safely; I got a clear look at him as I entered the house.

As I walked into the foyer, I found the investigation team waiting for me—Nolan, Alex, Tyler, and Zander. They related their experiences so far in the house, saying that they had heard footsteps above them and that their equipment had picked up some paranormal activity as well. I could immediately tell that they were anxious. They had already been investigating for a few hours; their cameras were set up and they had paranormal equipment spread out all over the ground floor. Nolan asked me if they could film a short piece about the house's history and, since my car was dead in the driveway anyway, I agreed to sit down with them. Almost immediately, I felt something come up behind me and touch the back of my neck. I didn't react outwardly—the team was anxious enough already and I didn't want to feed the entity any more energy. I was familiar with how it operated and I knew it would be a much smarter move to see how far it would go before I tried to wear it down.

"It's a lovely house, but you just can't live here," I said after Nolan announced that the cameras were rolling. Then I explained the rules of the house to the team. "Don't talk about your families, your animals, or your personal lives while you're here, because the information may be used against you. There's a dark force inside this house and it preys on people's emotions—especially anger, fear, and sadness." As we talked, I repeatedly saw a shadow out of the corner of my eye. I knew we were being watched, but I also knew that, if I gave the entity my attention, there would be consequences. It wanted my reaction to start a chain reaction—my emotions feeding into the team's emotions, turning us all into a spiritual power source for an entity who only wanted to feed off our energy. I felt in my bones that Kat was right; all of us were in danger in the house that night.

Nolan asked if they could film a séance to see which spirits would communicate with us. I agreed, but told them that, if at any time anything felt weird, I would shut it down. I told them that we couldn't provoke any type of negativity energy in the house, and that it would be best if they didn't think about deceased loved ones or pets. It was important, I stressed, that we go into the session with clear thoughts and that we project protection for everyone in the room. Everyone agreed, although Alex in particular seemed to notice how serious I was.

As soon as we began the séance and fired up the spirit box, a voice came through and very clearly said Nolan's name. The team were all amazed at how quickly his name had come through, as was I. At this point, I knew that Nolan had become the entity's target and that he would be the first to be hit by the house's energy. The room became freezing cold and a circle of chilling energy gathered around us in the dark. One of the team jumped, exclaiming that something had touched him. I began to hear heavy breathing as the spirit box started spitting out words at breakneck speed. I knew I needed a plan to keep everyone safe.

"I don't feel so good," Nolan said suddenly, his voice rising in pitch. "I have to get out of this house. My head, the pressure . . . my heart . . ." I reached over and grabbed him, frightening him with my sudden move. But I knew it wasn't me he had to worry about. I told him that he had to leave, that he was far too deeply into the energy. The other team members began to panic; I heard one of them say that something was wrong with Nolan's face, and that he wasn't Nolan any longer.

"Someone get him out of the house right now!" I ordered them. "Meet me outside on the street!"

As I left the Séance Room, I smelled a distinct odor of sulfur there. Once outside the house, I cleansed the team with kosher salt and holy oil to remove any negative energy that might be affecting them. I told them that the best thing they could do at the moment was to sit outside for a while. It was clear to me that the house was having a very active night. Bellaire House is both a living entity and a paranormal biodome teeming with supernatural energy. Sometimes when it gets in a mood, the best thing you can do is to leave it alone for a while. The safest place to be when the house is acting like this is outside of it.

After a little while, I realized that my son was going to need a ride home from his studio and I asked the team if they would feel comfortable staying outside in the yard while I went to pick him up. To my relief, my car started, leaving me to wonder as I drove away why it hadn't started earlier. Was I being summoned to help Nolan's team? Or was the house simply trying to submit me to another paranormal experience?

After I left, the team began to feel calmer and decided that they would go back inside to try to collect more data. They told me later that they spent the evening playing a knocking game, like the one used by the Fox sisters, two spiritualists who came to fame in the mid-1800s. They began by knocking to see if the spirits would imitate them. Unlike the Fox sisters, however, they didn't have much luck. It seems the house spirits were not amused by their game. Nor did they experience any EVP activity or any other unusual phenonmena. But things quickly changed when they began asking the spirits of the house verbal questions.

"Do you want us to leave the house?" Nolan asked.

The response came through as: "Edwin."

"Do you want us to stay the night?" Nolan continued.

As a draft of cold air blew through the house, they received another one-word response: "Stupid."

Alex asked the responding spirit to touch the green light on his K2 meter. An anamoly appeared and hovered over the meter for a moment before actually going inside it, leading the team to think that the spirits of the house were trying to get to know them and wanted to show them some activity to make them feel more comfortable. They hadn't yet learned that, at Bellaire House, it's when you feel comfortable, when your guard is down, that you are most vulnerable to negative energies. Perhaps the house had already broken them in; it often gets to know everything about you during your first night there. By your second night, it either tests you or attacks you—or both. And Nolan already knew that he was the entity's target.

Over their stay in Bellaire House, the team captured two intelligent EVPs during the daytime. One said: "Come inside"; the other came across as: "Don't tell him." At one point, Nolan decided to go off on his own to investigate the Altar Room. He reported that, within minutes of stepping inside the room, he felt very uneasy. The other investigators had gone into the Edwin Heatherington Room, where a flashlight turned on to let them know that Edwin was with them. At this point, Nolan concluded that the spirits in the house were playing games with them. When he asked them to stop, they responded with my name: "Kristin."

As I rejoined them for the night, the activity continued to ramp up. We saw a full-body apparition appear in the Séance Room. Nolan noticed it first, and the SLS camera—a camera specifically built for paranormal investigation that detects spirit forms that can't be seen with the naked eye—picked up the shape of a figure standing behind Zander. At one point, I felt a foreign energy enter my body; when I stood up, the SLS camera showed a figure sitting in my chair.

"Come here, Nolan," said the spirit. A few moments later, Nolan was able to capture the image of two figures seated at the séance table. It looked as if they were holding their own séance. We wondered if they wanted to join us in our session, or if, perhaps, they were stuck in a moment in time in one of the many séances that had been held in the house during Edwin's day—like a recording repeating itself.

It was very late when the séance ended, and I needed to go home and sleep. So I told the team that I would see them in the morning before they left to go back to New York. When I returned to the house the next day, I found them all sleeping on the living room floor surrounded by a circle of salt. I had told them that, if they felt unsafe or in need of extra protection, they should make a circle of salt around their sleeping area, since nothing negative can cross a salt circle. I can only imagine what transpired that night after I left that made them take my advice.

After the team left for their long drive home, I remained to clean up. While I was tidying, I heard Austin and Layne come into the house. I asked Austin if he wanted some coffee and "thanked" him again for scaring me the other night.

"What are you talking about?" Austin said, giving me a funny look. I thought he was teasing me again, so I reminded him about how he'd banged on the window of my car and called me an old chicken. His reply shook me to my core. "I was in the north end last night," he said. "I was never here."

I knew that I had seen Austin standing outside my car, but I could also tell by the look on his face that he wasn't teasing me this time. So what exactly had banged on my window that night? It was at that point that I decided that cleaning up could wait for another day until I had more backup in the house. I was done with Bellaire House yanking my chain for that day.

HELPFUL HINTS

If you ever feel as if you are in need of extra protection against the paranormal in a haunted location, one of the easiest and best ways to protect yourself is to make a salt circle. Take kosher salt and draw a wide circle around your sleeping space. Negative energies and entities cannot cross this circle, so it will help to ensure your safety.

CHAPTER 6

Footsteps in the Attic

If there's one room in Bellaire House that has held more fascination for paranormal investigators than any other, it is probably the attic. Even in the early days, when I was still searching for any reason besides the paranormal for why my new house felt so strange, it was hard for me to deny that there was something going on in the attic.

The attic is quite a large room, with wood floors and a high ceiling. I thought it might be perfect for a recording studio and, in a way, it is—although what I originally had in mind was to record music, not EVPs. The attic was where I first heard phantom footsteps, alerting me to the fact that we were not alone in the house. Despite all my early reservations—my attempts to convince myself that I was tired, that I was traumatized, that my new house was normal—it was clear from the start that there was something lurking up in the attic.

The Bellaire House attic has four gables, each of which contains a double window that is shuttered on both the inside and the outside. There is a long, dark cubby hole in the left wall that is deep enough for a person, or even several people, to hide. Through both our spiritual communication and our research into the house's history, we've come to believe that a number of African American slaves hid in this cubbyhole as part of their journey along the Underground Railroad. In fact, we know that Jacob Davis was a prominent Ohio abolitionist. Today, we can only imagine how frightening it must have been to have to hide in that attic, which was too hot in the summer and too cold in the winter, pressed together for safety, waiting silently for the chance to move toward freedom.

We now believe that an evil entity was already a resident of the attic when these runaways huddled there. Did they encounter it and its malice? What other horrors did it heap upon them? We know that one of the house's eleven portals opens within this cubbyhole and that, in many ways, the house is like a record player whose needle sometimes gets caught in the grooves of time, creating a sort of dimensional distortion in which energy imprints itself through traumatic events on the very fabric of the house's reality. The deeper the trauma, the deeper the groove. And the deeper the groove, the more the metaphoric needle skips.

The attic can be very warm during the summer months and there isn't any way to add a cooling system, so investigators working there during the summer must wear light clothing and avoid work during the hottest parts of the day. The lights in the ceiling no longer work, and we instruct visitors, for their own safety as well as the safety of the house, only to use the lamps we provide. I painted the attic walls blue in 2013 because, in an EVP session with Mike McCallister, the Gray Man indicated that, if the room were painted blue, he would be content to sit in his chair and look out the window at the river. To appease him, I acquiesced. But it was after I painted the attic that other spirits began to become quite noisy in their communications with us, as if, by granting this particular request, we had opened a door. From that point on, spirits were practically jumping in and out of the house's portals and the ley line beneath it.

A whole host of spirits and entities have been seen and experienced in the Bellaire House attic, but the ones who are seen most frequently are child spirits,

Emily Davis among them. I once saw Emily ascending the stairs to the attic, and it was in the attic that I first heard her voice through EVP communication. It was here that she first greeted me by name. Katrina Weidman, a paranormal investigator and star of the reality TV series *Paranormal Lockdown,* spoke of seeing a child in the attic even before she arrived at Bellaire House, and an investigator named Rebecca has repeatedly seen the ghost of a female child wearing an old-fashioned white gown. She probably wears this white nightgown because it is what she was wearing when she transitioned to spirit.

Child spirits are not the only spirits and entities we've encountered in the attic, however. This is where I had a two-hour conversation with the spirit of Captain John Fink, a riverboat captain who began mining and shipping coal in the 1830s. His spirit is just one of many that dwell within the house. The communication session I had with him was extraordinary, both because of its duration and because of the clarity with which his spirit spoke to me.

Another of the house's residents is the spirit of a servant we know as Mary, who has been haunting the attic for years. In 2007, when I was still living in the house, my cousin Karina was the first to see her. She had come to stay with me and chose to use the attic as her bedroom. One night, she came into my room looking frightened and told me that she'd woken up in the attic to find a woman standing over her bed. She described the woman, whom we later came to know as Mary, as an older lady with her hair in a bun wearing a flowing white nightgown and holding a candle. I have had a few communication sessions with Mary since in which she's told me that she doesn't want to leave Bellaire House because it is her home and that, in her earthly life, she watched over the house's women and children. Mary now keeps watch at night while people are asleep in the house so that the negative entity that lives in the attic doesn't "take the children." Many investigators who have visited the attic have been able to communicate with her, but when the evil entity is in control of the attic, she steers clear of it. She once told an investigator that, when the entity holds sway in the attic, she goes outside to do her chores until it leaves. During one session, Mary referred to me by my full name, saying: "Kristin Lee, my friend."

In July 2019, we witnessed a full apparition in the attic. A paranormal group had brought their entire team to the house to investigate for the weekend. They invited me to stay and even asked if I would facilitate a séance. I agreed. It turned out to be a very powerful session—one team member's grandmother came through, as did another's mother. Emily Davis also joined the conversation, introducing herself by name after greeting me as she always does, by saying: "Hi, Kristin!" Aaron, one of the investigators, was running a spirit box that, during the séance, began to turn on and off on its own. Whenever it turned on, the lights began to blink in rhythm with it. It was an incredibly intense session; at one point, I was nearly overwhelmed and found myself calling on five or six different energies at once. Luckily, my good friend Steve Hummel was there to step in and say the Lord's Prayer to rebalance the energy. After that, we took a break to ground and balance ourselves.

Afterward, a few of us ended up talking in Command Central—an observation station that was set up to monitor the most active rooms in the house using cameras. All of a sudden, I looked over and saw that something had been picked up on one of the cameras in the attic—an apparition of a woman sitting on the attic's couch. She reached over and placed her hand on a toy piano we had left up there. The piano, which we'd used earlier to coax the spirits to communicate, had an electronic keyboard with working lights. As the apparition's hand touched the keyboard, it lit up, as if a flesh-and-blood hand had been placed on it.

Paranormal Confessions

Once, we did an experiment in which we asked guests to pick a room in the house to investigate for an hour on their own to see if anyone could brave the house alone. A guest named Jay picked the attic. Allison, Jon, and I watched him on the DVR system in the foyer by the front door. Jay had his back to the cameras when we saw something pull his shirt to the side. A second later, it pulled his shirt to the other side. He jumped in fear and turned around, but there was nothing there. We couldn't see anything on the cameras, either. Whatever force had tugged on his shirt was quite invisible to the naked eye. When Jay came back downstairs, he told us that he had felt as if someone were "messing with him," that perhaps another investigator had been playing a prank on him. But he soon realized that he was completely alone in the attic. Startled, he left. When we reviewed the DVR footage with him, it clearly showed his shirt being tugged from side to side by invisible hands.

And that wasn't the only experience Jay had at Bellaire House. Earlier, using Steven Huff's portal, he'd had an hour-long conversation with his deceased mother. She was able to tell him that she loved him, that she was proud of him, and that she was always with him. It was a profound and emotional experience. Afterward, he and I cried together. To this day, I'm amazed and touched by the healing messages people have received from their loved ones in the afterlife.

The attic is not just the scene of harmless pranks and apparitions, however. A very disturbing pattern of activity occurs there that, to this day, shakes me to my core. When in the attic, you must be very careful of the windows that are set into the gables. As you approach them, you may feel a sense of foreboding. In 2008, when I still lived in the house, I was suffering from a bad flu and spent much of the time being sick in the first-floor bathroom. Sick as I was, I kept an ear out for the sounds of Layne playing with Bella. We were all sleeping on the first floor of the house at the time and I could hear the sound of Layne's feet and Bella's nails skittering across the hardwood floors as they made a game out of raiding the refrigerator and sharing the spoils. I had no reason to be worried; all the doors and windows were firmly locked, and Layne knew not to play outside without permission or to touch the stove. He was aware of all the usual childhood dangers that all good helicopter moms warn their children about. By this time, the attic door was always kept firmly locked, because we knew that there was something disturbing about the space even then—a sense that, when you were up there, you were not alone. I didn't want to have to worry about it, so I kept the door locked.

I didn't sense that anything was wrong until I realized that I could no longer hear Layne and Bella playing. No footsteps, no laughing, no barking. It was the kind of silence that makes a parent instantly alert. It had only been about a minute since I'd last heard them, but I nevertheless felt a nervousness creep up my spine and anxiety lit up my every nerve ending. My intuition told me that something was amiss.

"Layne, where are you?" I called, dragging my sick body out of the bathroom. "Bella, come!" Silence. I raced around the first floor looking for them, but they weren't there—not in the kitchen, not in the foyer, not in the hall. I ran up the stairs to the second floor as quickly as I could, willing them to be around every corner. It had only been a minute, after all.

Suddenly, in my left ear, I heard a voice whisper, so quietly that it was barely audible: "Attic." That was all. But that was all I needed to hear. I ran to the attic. Somehow the door at the bottom of the stairs had become unlocked, although it shouldn't have been possible for Layne to open it. I almost flew up the steps and, when I got to the top, my heart almost stopped. Layne was standing on the edge of the gable, ready to jump out the window.

"I'm Buzz Lightyear," he said. "I'm going to fly!"

I grabbed the back of his sleeper just as he said "fly" and caught him, pulling him away from the open window. Then I had a full-fledged panic attack and called my mother to come and get us out of the house. We didn't return for quite a while after that. It was a turning point for me. Up to that point, I had tried to rationalize my strange experiences in the house— the phantom footsteps, the ghostly apparitions. I knew that I had been through an incredible amount of trauma losing my previous home, but I was pretty sure that what I was experiencing here wasn't related to post-traumatic stress. The house, I had to conclude, was pure evil. I knew that, if I stayed there, it was going to hurt me and my family.

And this wasn't the only incident involving the attic windows. Several investigators have reported hearing voices telling them to go to the window, almost as if there is a spirit or an entity in the attic that wants to lure people to their deaths by convincing them to leap from the attic gables. At least one investigator reported that something told her to go to the window and jump. In my research into the house, I discovered that an old village rumor claimed that a servant's child had been lured to the attic and subsequently died by plunging from a window. On another occasion, a spirit communicated to us that his son had fallen from an attic gable to his death.

Steven Huff also received spirit communication in the attic that had something to do with a child and a special bloodline. What bloodline this might be remains a mystery. If the communication referred to the Heatherington bloodline, then it should be noted that there are no records of either Edwin or Lyde having any children of their own, although we know that there were children born to servants who lived in Bellaire House.

I have received an impression that the attic is a place where you could hide a child—perhaps one born out of wedlock, a "family secret" if you will—but this is only a feeling the house has given me that is backed up by old rumors. Nothing like this has ever been substantiated or proven. In any event, it seems likely to me, with my knowledge of the phenomena that occur in the house, that something traumatic involving a child did happen in the attic and that the house continually attempts to recreate this episode—an example of the "record skipping" yet again. The question is, did the entity in the attic cause this tragedy in the first place, or is it just determined to repeat it? So when venturing into the Bellaire House attic, take care, follow the rules—and stay well away from the windows.

HELPFUL HINTS

It's important to protect yourself spiritually when visiting Bellaire House or any other haunted location. Be sure to wear amulets—iron or silver are especially effective for guarding against negative energy or malicious spirits and entities. After returning home from a haunted location, take off your shoes and fill a bath with warm water and kosher salt. Swish your feet back and forth in the salt water to remove any negative energy that might be tracked into your own home.

Paranormal Confessions

CHAPTER 7

Crossing Over

The spiritual population of Bellaire House is so vast that it needs its own paranormal census. The house is home to many spirits, from many different backgrounds—not just the Heatheringtons, our two Emily Davises, and other nonhuman entities, but also the spirits of escaped African American slaves who lived during the Civil War and before. Although Ohio may not be the first state we think of when discussing the Underground Railroad, it was, in fact, home to a system of safehouses and hiding places designed to ferry escaped slaves to freedom, and this network played an important part in the state's history.

We know that Jacob Davis, the founder of Bellaire, was one of many prominent abolitionists who played a vital role in Ohio's Underground Railroad. Although

Bellaire House wasn't built until 1847, it stands on land that is honeycombed by a series of secret tunnels and passageways that very likely were used to help slaves escape to freedom. In fact, in our paranormal research within the house, we've often made contact with the spirits of slaves. The basement, near where the entrance to one of these tunnels is now walled up, is a particular hotspot of activity. It's always been very important to me to respect and honor these spirits, and to offer them whatever help I can. For instance, they don't like to be referred to as "slaves"; they've made this known during many spiritual communications. Instead, we refer to them as "servants," and it's very important to us that visitors to the house do the same.

In September 2018, when a group of us were investigating the attic, the house was being particularly active. A 3-D camera had caught an image of a spirit standing next to an investigator. It looked as if it were touching her, but she said she didn't feel any spiritual energy nearby. Jon and I also heard the disembodied voice of a young female child who was humming. Although we looked all around the attic trying to pinpoint the source of the sound, we couldn't. Then, later that night, we communicated with a group of spirits of servants who were trapped inside the house. They made it very clear to us that they wanted to leave, but couldn't without assistance. We spent about an hour discussing it before we came up with a plan—we would help these spirits cross over to the afterlife.

I had never before worked with a group to help spirits cross over—either at Bellaire House or elsewhere. But I now felt that it needed to be done. After all, these spirits had expressed a desire to leave, and it's unethical to keep any spirit bound to a location against its will. Moreover, one of my biggest fears is that, once I myself transition to spirit, my energy will become trapped in the house. I have always felt that, because I have become such a big part of the research into the house and its history, it would only be natural for me to end up there after I transition. My greatest fear is that, like so many other spirits in the house, I will become ruled by the entity in the house—controlled like a puppet on strings. I've tried for years to cast out this fear, but I've yet to find anything that completely reassures me that, when I cross over, I will not be trapped inside Bellaire House.

We kept the group for the crossing-over rite small—just me, Jon, Allison, and Layne. As we walked to the attic, Layne took me by the arm and pulled me into the office area, which is located directly below the attic and has a window that leads to the roof. As he clutched my wrist tightly, he said: "What are we doing? This is crazy. I get that we need to help the servants, but what if that thing comes for us?" He was worried that the attic entity would overcome us. "Your back is so bad sometimes you can't walk!" he reminded me. "Jon has a bad back, too, and Allison is about ninety pounds soaking wet!"

I asked Layne if he wanted to go home, assuring him that, if he was nervous, he could sit this one out. He replied that he would stay, but that he had a bad feeling. He told me that, since in all likelihood he would outlive Jon and I, he felt that he had to learn how to help a spirit cross over in case he had to act for us one day. "It could be any one of us trapped in this house," he said, "and I don't want to spend my afterlife here." We took a moment to steady ourselves, then he added: "I'm going to be texting Daniel while we do this. If anything bad happens, we may need backup to get us all out of this stupid house!"

Once in the attic, I made a circle of coarse kosher salt to protect us all. Inside the circle, I blessed all our heads with holy oil. Everyone present was wearing Strega oil for protection as well. We sat close to each other; we all knew to keep an eye on everyone else in the room and we were mindful of each other's safety. We were also watching for anything from within the house that might try to prevent us from helping the servant spirits cross over. We all understood that what we were undertaking was potentially dangerous, and that, in order to succeed, we needed to calm our nerves and clear our minds.

To begin, we called upon San Miguel and the positive spirits who resided in the house to assist us in the rite. Jon asked for the name of a spirit so we could identify whom we were helping. We received a response, but not in the form of a spirit's name. We heard: "Layne . . . wossie," which led us to believe that the spirits were reacting to Layne's fear.

"Can you see us?" I asked.

"Alfred," came the response. "Others."

"Can you tell us the name of someone who is present?" asked Allison.

"Charles," came the response. "Malicious."

Suddenly, a spirit we'd previously identified as that of a woman named Sarah came through and said: "I want freedom!"

"Freedom," echoed the voice that belonged to Charles. "The light. I want to go to the light."

"Where are you?" I asked Sarah and Charles. "What room are you in? Can you see the river?" The house is very close to the Ohio River and, on a clear night, you can watch the moon rise over it. It's a beautiful sight.

"River," the spirits repeated back to us. "See, river. You should know what I see!"

I told the spirits to leave the house and walk to the river; no one would stop them, they were in no danger, and there would be no retaliation. Allison began to recite the Lord's Prayer as Jon continued to tell the spirits to walk out of the house. Someone said the name "Lucien" as I asked Sarah and Charles to tell me what they were seeing.

"Beautiful scenery," came the response.

That was when Mary identified herself to us and said: "They are leaving." Jon asked Mary to touch the REM pod and she said: "No. I help get them out." A few seconds later, Mary added: "No time for games. I love you, son. Leave. Go. River. Get on the boat."

Another spirit came through and said: "Sarah! Out! Leave! Run!"

"My flesh is your flesh," said another spirit, one whom I could not identify. "I am guilty."

None of us understood this message. We kept asking: "Who is guilty?"

"Allison," came the response. This was even more puzzling. When Layne asked what Allison was guilty of, the response was: "I don't know. She's praying." A few seconds later, a spirit said: "The wolf." Then we heard a name: "Mary Allen."

"Mary Allen, I am sorry," said a spirit. "Sin. Forgive me. I am leaving. Come and find me."

As the spirit said this, the attic door began to open slowly. A spirit chimed in with: "Let us know what he says."

"Can you tell us where you are?" I asked. A spirit replied that they were in the basement. I asked if they were seeking their freedom.

"Yes," came the response. "You should get on with her."

I told this spirit to go to the river with Mary and Charles, and that Captain Fink's boat was waiting for them. I told them that they needed to get on the boat, that they would be safe as they waited for the others. I needed them to understand that we were in another time now, not in the dimension of their own earthly lives, and that all of us were there to help them move on. I told them that they were not in any danger and that they were free. I told them they needed to move on toward their freedom.

A female spirit came in and said: "Kristin, remember us. There it is, there is our freedom!"

"I'm nervous," said another spirit.

"She is scared," said a male spirit. "Kristin, where is Huff?" referring to Steven Huff. Ever since Steven had first come to Bellaire House, the spirits there had often requested him by name.

The spirits then began to have a conversation among themselves about leaving the house.

"I wish she would get on with it," one said. Then: "I am nervous, help me . . . you should go. The house is original. Lucien, help me get out of this. Will miss you. Leave us. My eyes are very alert. Mommy, Mommy. Sarah is the source. I'll leave. Wolf. I want to go home."

I knew that this was the final chance to get as many of these spirits out of the house as I could. Before I even realized that I'd opened my mouth, I said: "The boat is on the river! Go to the river! Go to your freedom!"

We heard a voice say: "I'll listen."

I repeated to them that they were safe and that no one would stop them.

"The light," said a voice. "Peace."

Suddenly, I heard a low growl. The energy in the attic started to shift, and it became darker—not just the energy, but also the light. It was as if a shadow had fallen over us.

A new voice came through: "You are mine forever."

"No!" I screamed. "Servants, you are safe! You must leave now to claim your freedom. Go to the river!" It was clear that we didn't have much more time. Jon said that he felt sick, and Allison had started to rock back and forth. Layne told me to be careful and not to become too emotional. Then he addressed the spirits:

"Please go to the river. You can leave Bellaire. You can go back home or to heaven and see your families, but you need to go before the danger takes over. Please run to the river now!"

"I will be careful," we heard a spirit say.

Immediately after that, Eliza came through. She said both my name and Layne's, then she said: "Leave. Leave now. He is coming!"

"We have to close this session," said Jon. The energy inside the house was surging, visibly affecting all of us. "We've got one minute to get out of this house. We're in danger!" Allison was still rocking back and forth—speaking, but incoherently. The words that were flowing from her lips were not in any language I recognized. I knew that Jon was right that we were in danger and that we had to get out of the house as quickly as possible. It was Layne who finally broke the circle, announcing his intention to San Miguel before he acted. He and Jon got Allison through the door and, together, carried her out of the house. I stayed for a moment, alone in the silence of the house.

"Go to the river," I kept saying. "You have to leave now. Please go to the river and let me know that you're there. I'm in danger; I have to leave this house. Please hurry and come with me now!" At this point, Layne ran back into the house looking for me. I met him in the Séance Room and, together, we hurried out the front door. I said nothing aloud, but I had already made it clear to the spirits that, if they wanted their freedom, they could follow me away from the confines of Bellaire House. Taking a deep breath, I shut the door behind Layne and myself.

We went to the bottom of the yard to join Allison and Jon. Allison was crying from a mixture of sadness and the overload of energy we had experienced. I had a bottle of Strega oil with me and I used it to bless her. All of us sat together for a long moment. Then, in the distance, we heard a boat blow its horn ten times. When we heard this, we all thought that perhaps some of the spirits had made it to the river after all. I hoped that they had crossed over safely and that they were now at peace with their families.

We were all exhausted. No one had the energy to go back into the house that night. Instead, we lay on the grass, just staring up at the house as it loomed against the night sky. Eventually, Jon pulled out his pocket ghost box and asked: "How many spirits got on the boat tonight? Are they on their way to freedom?"

The answer that came back was clear as day: "Ten." Indeed, the boat horn that we'd heard had sounded ten times. I felt relieved at this confirmation, believing that we had helped ten spirits cross over that night. As we continued to stare up at the house, we saw purple lights coming out of the attic. I believe that these lights were energy—energy that was leaving the house for elsewhere. This was all the confirmation I needed to know that, at least for that night, our jobs were done.

HELPFUL HINTS

Helping spirits cross over to the afterlife is a big undertaking, but a worthwhile one. To be successful, it helps to have a spiritual rapport with the spirits. You can talk to them as a way to build up this rapport. It's important to honor these spirits and to treat them with dignity and respect. Always remember that these earthbound spirits were once someone's friends, someone's family. Honor them as you would your own friends and family. This is very draining work. If you feel you must attempt it, do not do so alone. Enlist the help of someone who is experienced! Do not try to do this yourself under any circumstances.

CHAPTER 8

The Star People and the Secrets of Ormus

Earthbound spirits and nonhuman entities aren't the only paranormal beings that have made contact with us in Bellaire House. Between the abandoned coal mine, sacred Shawnee burial caves, and a powerful astrological alignment in the night sky, the house sits between two great wells of spiritual power, bringing a whole new meaning to the phrase: As above, so below.

One evening in the summer of 2016, Mike Simpson and I led a séance together. Mike leads a large ghost-hunting company and has helped conduct investigations at many notable haunted locations throughout Indiana, Ohio, Pennsylvania, and West Virginia. He's also given hundreds of presentations about Bellaire House over the years. He's one of the best paranormal investigators I've ever had the pleasure of knowing and I was very excited to be conducting this séance with him. But I never in a million years could have predicted how that night would go or with what we would communicate—an entity or entities who identified themselves as "star people." We commonly refer to them as aliens, extraterrestrials, or ultraterrestrial beings.

It was not our intention on that night to make contact with these star people. Our goal was to communicate with Edwin and Lyde. I was hopeful that some Native American spirits from the land might come through as well. I led the séance and Mike assisted me, not knowing that, through a variety of paranormal equipment, we had unwittingly created a supernatural platform for intergalactic communication. I had never even imagined that we might achieve communication with extraterrestrial beings.

The location of Bellaire House is very special, astrologically speaking. If you ever visit the house, I highly recommend taking some time away from the ghosts to look up at the night sky. It's a perfect location to view constellations like Ursa Major, Ursa Minor, Andromeda, Draco, Cygnis, and Capricorn. You can also clearly see a planetary alignment between Mars, Saturn, Mercury, Venus, and Jupiter. It's very possible that this concentration of power has contributed to the house's incredible level of paranormal activity, as this is a perfect planetary alignment to manifest any human desire. As it turns out, it's also a way to tap into galactic portals to communicate with intelligent beings.

We began the séance by asking some of our more typical investigatory questions to test what was coming through for us. When participating in a séance, it is important to remain focused and direct with your line of inquiry. Your questions must be clear to the spirits on the Other Side; say what you mean, not what you think would sound good if you were in a movie. We started by asking who the current president was and received "Obama" as a response. (Remember, this happened in the summer of 2016.) Then we asked who the next president would be. The reply came: "Not the women." When we asked if they could see us, the reply was clear and positive: "Yes, we are with you."

One of the first clues I had that we were communicating, not with an earthbound spirit, but rather with beings of a higher intergalactic intelligence was the duration of our session. Earthbound spirits typically lose energy after about five minutes of communication. It's hard for them to sustain communication with humans for longer than that. During this séance, however, we communicated with the star people for more than two hours! The energy remained extremely high and powerful the whole time; the star people did not appear to have an issue sustaining prolonged communication with us.

We asked if a war was coming and the reply we got was chilling: "Human war. Death." We asked how we, as humans, could stop this war and they replied: "Harmony. Love. Music. Peace." When we asked how we, as people, could become better humans, we received a very similar response: "Love. Harmony. Peace." We asked what we could do to save the Earth, and again the response came through: "Love. Peace." We asked what we could we do to stop the war. They said: "Love over greed and hatred."

When we asked who started the war, the star people replied with one word: "Dawn." It wasn't clear whether they were referring to dawn as the time of day, or whether they perhaps meant dawn more metaphorically, as in the dawning of a new age. It's also possible that they were referring either to a person named Dawn or to someone whose name sounds like Dawn. This is a good example of how, while we must always strive to be clear and concise during a séance, communications from other realms may not always be easy to understand. Think of it as a game of telephone. By the time the answer comes through to us, it has passed through different dimensions and energies, so it may be difficult for us to glean the exact meaning.

We asked: "Will there be deaths?" The answer came back: "Millions die." We asked: "How do we sustain life?" Again the star people replied: "Harmony, love, and peace." When we asked what we could do to live a longer life, the star people replied: "Ormus."

I discovered later that ormus, also known as "white powder gold," is gold that is spiritually charged with amazing healing powers. It is a superconductor that is believed to exist partially in another dimension. Ancient alchemists produced this material only for the most privileged—priests and pharaohs. It's said that they ingested it to increase their mental clarity, to strengthen their awareness of the life force all around them, and to gain wisdom and a deep understanding of the universe. Ormus allegedly assists and repairs the body's natural communication between body, mind, and spirit, making it a rejuvenating substance with amazing healing potential. Some even believe that it can help repair damaged DNA. Although there are online sites that claim to sell ormus, I never recommend ingesting any unknown substance. Moreover, if you have an underlying condition, it's important that you speak to your doctor before taking any new supplement—especially one recommended by aliens.

Next, I heard the word "Egyptian" coming in from the spirit box. Everyone in our group was pumped and amped up by the energy that was circulating around us. Some were crying from the emotional overload we were experiencing, while others were getting direct and personal messages from the extraterrestrials. Personally, I felt like Wonder Woman—as if I could lift a car and throw it across the yard! It was an incredible sensation. It was difficult for all of us to wrap our heads around what we were experiencing and understand that we had tapped into some kind of extraterrestrial power. Before that night, many of us hadn't even believed that such beings existed. Yet here we were, talking to them! And not just communicating; they were clearly and directly answering our questions. We *felt* the proof of alien life that night.

Mike took over the questioning as many in the group were overwhelmed by the energy present. Mike has a smooth and encouraging style when communicating with spirits and is amazingly skilled at opening dialogue with the beyond. He asked: "With the ormus, how long can we live?" The star people replied: "160 to 180 years." Then they said: "Noah." It seems likely to me that they were referring to the biblical Noah, who is reported to have had a much longer lifespan than we have today. Moreover, the fact that the star people mentioned Noah instantly intrigued me. Following that thread, I asked: "Will there be another flood?" I was referring, of course, to the great biblical flood that prompted Noah to gather two of every animal into his ark. The star people replied: "Yes." When I asked when, they said: "2020."

We asked how we could cure cancer. The reply came: "Ormus early." Ormus again! We asked what the next thing was that will kill humans. The star people answered: "Flu." When we asked when, they replied: "2019. Effects many." When we asked what we could do to help the victims, they said: "Live rural. Stay inside. Zinc and ormus." Then they added: "Love. Sing. Music. Harmony. Peace." They repeated "music" and "sing" several times: "Sing, sing, sing. Music, music, music."

Because of the incredible duration of our session, what they told us, and the ways they conveyed that information—and because of how we felt during the communication and the fact that they referred to themselves as "star people"—I truly believe that we were communicating with a being or beings of higher intelligence. Furthermore, I believe that it was their intention to guide us through an uncertain future. What a profound experience! Mike and I both still have a very hard time wrapping our heads around what we experienced that night. It's hard to accept that there truly is a higher level of intelligence, even when you've communicated with it directly. It was a different experience entirely from communicating with earthly spirits. Perhaps these star people exist outside of time or experience time differently, or perhaps we communicated with beings who were literally from the future. But no matter their nature, it felt as if they had information about the future that they wanted to share with us.

That night, these beings acted like a universal oracle, warning us so that we could better prepare for our own future. I was touched, both spiritually and emotionally, by the level of trust they exhibited. It seems to me that the star people saw the good in us and trusted us with this information so that we could continue to better ourselves as we strive for a brighter future. It was a completely incredible, out-of-this-world experience—literally! I remained on a paranormal high for about three months after that night. I dove into researching ormus and star people, hungry for information that could help me better understand and contextualize what we had experienced.

Since our communication with the star people, I have seen UFOs in the sky above my house several times. My current home is about seven miles away from Bellaire House, in the Bellaire Hills behind it. The view there is amazing; on a clear night, I can see planets with my naked eye. The first time I saw a UFO, however, was around nine or ten in the morning. I was sitting in my sun room with my dog Ani, named after Ani DiFranco. She was looking out the window when, suddenly, she lunged up and started barking at the sky. As I tried to calm her down, I looked around to see what had startled her. That was when I saw the UFO. It looked like a brilliant silver orb that darted in and out of the sky. It was amazing; I had never seen anything like it.

I waited breathlessly for it to reappear, because I wanted to see exactly what it was. Could it be a weather balloon? I didn't think so, because it was too high in the sky. I looked for a vapor trail from an airplane, but the sky was clear. I saw the object peaking in and out of the sky two or three times before I finally called for my husband to come see it. And that's when it disappeared, almost as if it knew that I had called for another witness. I was disappointed, but still excited by what I had seen. The next time I saw a UFO was about eighteen months later. Like the first one, this brilliant object darted in and out of the sky, occasionally disappearing behind the clouds, then reappearing. It remained visible for about an hour before vanishing.

HELPFUL HINTS

If there are UFOs in the sky above you and you do not wish to make contact with extraterrestrial beings of any sort, or if you fear alien abduction, you may want to invoke spiritual protection. A popular Mexican tradition entails making or commissioning small paintings called *retablos* or *laminas* that depict miraculous events. Retablos are used to thank saints for many acts of salvation, including protection from alien abduction! Traditionally, they are created on thin sheets of tin or other inexpensive metal using oil paints. Many retablos are commissioned from professional retablo artists, known as *retableros* (makers of retablos) or *milagreros* (makers of miracles), who consider their art a sacred occupation. If you cannot commission a retablo, you can make one for yourself.

The primary sacred beings invoked for protection from extraterrestrials and UFOs are El Niño de Atocha, a manifestation of the Christ Child, Our Lady of Guadalupe, and Our Lady of San Juan de Los Lagos, as well as San Miguel (Archangel Michael), Saint Barbara, Saint Charbel, and Martin de Porres. If you have a favorite saint or deity to whom you often look for protection, you may invoke them as well.

A retablo usually depicts the moment when a miracle occurred. For example, someone rescued from a flood may show their thanks by painting a retablo that depicts them escaping the rising waters. Your retablo should depict the saint or sacred being you invoked keeping you safe from danger. If, for example, you are thankful that you have not been chosen to help ET get home, you may paint your deity or saint hovering in the air between your home and a flying saucer. Write what you are thankful for on your retablo. Finished retablos are often brought to religious shrines as testimonials or placed on home altars. If you have a home altar, you can put your homemade retablo there.

CHAPTER 9

The Bishop Pays a Visit

By 2015, Bellaire House had been in my possession for ten years. After my terrifying experiences within it, I no longer felt comfortable living there, but, as any homeowner knows, it can be a very difficult thing to divest yourself of a piece of property—especially one that comes with a reputation. So I decided to rent the house. The tenants never stayed very long, however. The spirits always asserted themselves, chasing them away and leaving me with a haunted house on my hands. After the last tenants left in 2015, I felt down-trodden and was overcome with anxiety. I worried that my days were numbered because of the energies that resided in the house and knew that I had to make a powerful change—for good, this time. But I knew I needed some serious spiritual help to accomplish this. That was when I asked Bishop James Long to make a house call.

I first met Bishop Long when he came to Bellaire House with Kat Lang, a petite woman from Seattle who is the director of the Paranormal Clergy. Born in Louisville, Kentucky, the bishop knew from a young age that he had a calling to the priesthood. I remember him once telling me that, when he was a child, his mother had asked what he wanted to be when he grew up. They were in church at the time, and James pointed to the priest and said: "I want to do what he does."

Bishop Long serves as a bishop of the United States Old Catholic Church. He has earned a reputation for offering expert spiritual help to all those who seek his guidance. I first became aware of his work in 2008 when Mike and Amanda McCallister, who worked with Ohio Valley Paranormal Research and Investigation (OVPRI), began coming to Bellaire House. Mike frequently told the negative entities inside the house that he was going to "call a bishop" to expel them. Whenever this happened, we received feedback from our paranormal equipment that indicated that the entities hated the idea, because validly ordained priests can perform exorcisms if they are given permission by their bishop to do so. The entities in the house knew that this could result in them being permanently expelled, or even sent back to hell.

I got to know Bishop Long through his ministry for the homeless. He was the most spiritually powerful man I knew, and I decided to reach out to him and ask him to hold an event at Bellaire House to raise money for homeless families. I explained to him that there was so much paranormal activity in the house that the kitchen doors often opened all by themselves and that the telephone, although disconnected, rang at all hours. I described how the house's heavy doors frequently slammed themselves shut, and that one tenant had left after a chandelier fell, barely missing his head. I knew I was standing on a dangerous threshold and asked him to come to the house to help me and my family. I knew I was at the riskiest point of my life, and I had every reason to be afraid.

On his last investigation at the house, Mike McCallister had collected a truly chilling EVP recording. Certain that the negative entity was targeting me directly, he asked it: "What do you want with Kristin?" The reply was very clear: "I'm going to kill her." When Mike heard that, he threw the recorder across the room and started shouting at the entity. He said that a bishop would soon arrive to deal with all the negative energies in the house.

It was years later, however, that Bishop Long arrived at the house with his assistant investigator, Kat Lang. As a person who is deeply sensitive to energies, she, like me, is a survivor of paranormal activities and she uses what she has learned from those experiences to counsel families who are experiencing hauntings. When we first met, Kat asked me a series of questions about my own experiences to test their authenticity, and we developed a deep understanding of each other that became the basis of a strong friendship.

After touring the house for the first time, Bishop Long wrote me a detailed letter about his experiences. He hadn't watched any of the TV shows in which the house was featured, because he didn't want them to influence his personal thoughts about the property. He wrote that he had begun to feel a heaviness as he toured the first floor, a weighty sensation that became more intense as he got closer to the stairs that led to the second floor. He reported having the same feeling in other demonic cases with which he had dealt in the past. The heaviness continued to grow with each step he climbed, and he sensed that he was in the presence of something that did not want him there. As he reached the top of the stairs, an invisible force shoved him, trying to push him back down. It was clear that his presence was not welcome.

As the bishop started his investigation of the second floor, he was immediately drawn to the Edwin Heatherington Room, where the entity had attacked me years before. The bishop set up several recording devices, one of which recorded the following words: "Bishop. Leave. Demon. Dark." Everyone involved in the bishop's investigation that day experienced some kind of acute paranormal phenomenon. Thankfully, despite the attempt made on the bishop at the top of the stairs, no one was hurt. Suffice it to say that the bishop was now well aware of the dangers that the house presented.

Bishop Long and I agreed that we would cohost a two-day event at the house to raise money for the homeless. The event would consist of his demonology and angelology classes, as well as a special seminar on how to combat demonic possession. Four hours after posting the event, it was fully subscribed and we raised over $1,700 for homeless families. Prior to the bishop's arrival, a group of paranormal investigators conducted an EVP session and I told an entity that the bishop would arrive soon. It responded in a clear sentence: "I hate the bishop." The quality of the communication was a clear Class A, the highest rating on the scale. The demon started screaming: "Bishop! Bishop James Long! Bishop! Bishop James Long! Bishop!

Bishop James Long!" It repeated these ravings three times, perhaps mocking the Catholic Trinity. It was clearly threatened by the bishop, knowing he would not back down from a face-to-face encounter with a demon.

You can imagine how anxious I was to expel this entity. But, as the saying goes, when it rains it pours. As we were setting up for the bishop's seminar, my husband arrived to tell me that Layne had suffered a fall at his Grandma Honey's house. As we stood in the driveway talking about the accident, Daniel specifically told me that he had taken Layne's pills. Later, as I attended the bishop's session with the rest of the guests, the entity kept saying: "Daniel. Daniel. Aquarius. Drummer. Pills. Honey." I was the only person in the room who knew about the conversation my husband and I had had in the driveway. It simply wasn't possible that any earthly beings had overheard us. But, apparently, the entity had been listening. In that moment, I felt very frightened and very intimidated, knowing that I was being singled out and personally threatened with the fact that the demon had overheard my conversation with my husband.

All of a sudden, Kat pulled me close. "They're messing with you," she whispered. "Our God is bigger than this storm. Keep repeating this to yourself and turn this evil nonsense out of your head right now!" I knew she was right and that the entity was testing my willpower, but it was hard to shift my focus away from what the demon was saying when it was so clearly aimed at me. Kat leaned closer and said: "Listen to me now. My God is bigger than this storm." As she said it, she squeezed my hand lightly with each syllable. I took a deep breath and began repeating the mantra in my head: "My God is bigger than this storm. My God is bigger than this storm."

It worked; the entity turned away from me and began to repeat the names of other women. Later, we discovered that all these women had two things in common: they were all related to the people attending the session, and they were all women who had died of cancer. This greatly upset one guest, who started to cry. Kat led me over to the tearful woman and asked me to stand on one side of her while she stood on the other. I knew what I had to do. I continued reciting my mantra: "My God is bigger than this storm!"

When the bishop ended the session, he asked Kat to take the guests into another room. I closed and locked the door behind them, leaving me alone with the bishop. I asked him to bring out the entity that had held me down in bed and thrown Bella up against the wall that terrible night. I wanted to regain control of my life, and I knew that, if I were going to continue to own Bellaire House, I had to conquer this fear. And

I couldn't overcome it without expelling that demon. Bishop Long asked me if I was sure and I said: "Yes." He told me that, once we got started, I would have to follow his instructions without question. He made me promise that I would not veer off the spiritual path he laid out, no matter what happened. I agreed and we started the rite.

The bishop sat under the window, near the bed where the entity had held me down, while I sat with my back against the door. "Show yourself!" he commanded. Then he began speaking in Latin as he ordered the entity to reveal itself. He started by reciting the Lord's Prayer, the Hail Mary, and the Glory Be prayers. As he prayed, I saw a black mass resembling a static-filled rain cloud come out of the wall in the corner and move toward me. Every muscle in my body tensed. I could hear the bishop talking, but he began to sound very far away, as if his voice were coming through a tunnel. Suddenly, I heard him say: "Kristin, listen to me now!" It was as if I had snapped back to myself; my hearing returned to normal and the bishop's voice no longer seemed muffled.

"Do you see it?" asked the bishop.

"Yes!" I said, staring at the looming mass.

I felt as if I were locked in a meat freezer. A cold rush blew through me and I felt filled with electrical shocks. The entity was now right in front of me, and

I became aware that beads of cold sweat were running down my face. In spite of all of this, however, I felt charged—strong enough to lift up the entire Bellaire House and throw it across the Ohio River. I could hear the bishop speaking in Latin. The device we had set up to capture the entity's response was speaking as well. It said: "One blessed be dog!"

I had heard this phrase before. When Mike and Amanda McCallister had been investigating at the house in 2009, the entity had repeated that phrase over and over in that very room to mock me, to disturb me, so it could use my emotions against me. It was talking about my beloved dog Bella. She had given birth to seven puppies in that room, and it had been a very emotional experience for me. I had previously been told that she couldn't have puppies and I wasn't able to be with her for the birth due to a work commitment that had called me away. A friend of mine helped with the delivery in my stead. It was a difficult birth, and two of the pups didn't survive. Both myself and others had long known that the evil entity had been behind the death of the pups, and it was all too happy to take the credit. That voice had haunted me for years, but this time it was different. I had the bishop's help and I wasn't going to let the entity win.

"One blessed be dog," repeated the entity. Then it started ranting: "Demon, demon, demon!" once again repeating words three times to disrespect the Catholic Trinity in front of the bishop. I was stunned into silence. I had been through so much in the house—things I could never have imagined in a million years—and yet I had never experienced anything quite like this before. I could see that there was a spiritual war going on between the bishop and the demon, and I knew that I was either a trigger, or perhaps just bait. It made me nervous not to be an active participant; I wasn't exactly sure what I was supposed to do. I opened my mouth several times to tell the bishop that I had heard the phrase "One blessed be dog" before, but I was always cut off by something. All I could get out was: "But Bishop, I need to tell you something!"

Bishop Long wasn't listening to me, however. He was using all of his power to fight the demon. Suddenly, the door started to open with a slow, rusty, creaking noise. It remained open a moment before it blew shut with the most powerful force I had ever felt inside the house. I screamed and I think I must have jumped two or three inches straight up in the air. I could feel the energy change immediately. With that hellish slam of the door, it was finally all over. The demon was expelled!

I was left speechless. I wanted someone to pinch me to make sure it hadn't been a dream, that I was awake and had really witnessed everything that had just happened. Had I not been with the bishop, I truly believe my life would have been in danger. I was so happy that he and I were still alive and in one piece. We'd survived the wrath of the entity and shoved it back where it belonged—right to hell. The bishop was tired after the rite and had to leave to restore his energy. However, when Kat was done with the second session, I took her aside to tell her everything that had occurred—not just in the rite, but also before it when the demon had targeted me by repeating: "Daniel. Drummer. Aquarius." You see, my husband, Daniel, is both a drummer and an Aquarius.

When Kat realized the severity of the situation, she said: "You are going to need a lot of help here. What can I do to help you?"

"Don't leave me here alone," I begged her. "Teach me so I can help show other families that there is a light at the end of this tunnel." Feeling more confident, I added: "Together, we can survive these experiences."

From that day on, I started working for the greater good of Bellaire House. Whenever I needed help, I knew I had friends like Bishop Long and Kat Lang to call on for support. Kat even moved to Bellaire to help me operate the house under the guidance and protection of the Old Catholic Church. Witnessing that exorcism had given me the strength and courage to move forward and made me believe that the evil in the house could be conquered. Finally, I could feel that things were going in the right direction and that good things were just around the corner.

The event that Bishop Long and I conducted at Bellaire House was a massive success. To my surprise, a year later, television producers began calling for my story and asking for my permission to feature the house on multiple shows. Finally, the notorious Bellaire House was converted into an afterlife research center—a platform for research and for communication with the entities of the beyond to help unlock the mysteries of the universe.

HELPFUL HINTS

Kat Lang taught me a trick that I like to use when I meet new people. She told me that, before entering a meeting, I should soak my hands in holy water, then let them air-dry without toweling them off. She also taught me that, if someone refuses to shake your hand without a good reason, it may mean that they have something to hide. While it is true that some people do not shake hands because of their personal, spiritual, or religious beliefs (and this should always be respected), or perhaps because they are concerned about germs, if someone won't shake your hand after a good soak in holy water, you may want to avoid that person! As an alternative to holy water, you can make yourself a handwash using kosher salt dissolved in water. Say your preferred spiritual blessing over the water, then use it to wash your hands. The combination of kosher salt and your personal blessing will make the water holy to you!

CHAPTER 10

Ghostly Assaults

Many types of spirits exist within the walls of Bellaire House, and they all have different motivations and desires. Some are earthly spirits reaching out to communicate with the living, while others are distinctly nonhuman in their energy. One type of spirit, a male entity known as an incubus, feeds off sexual energy. An incubus, according to traditional beliefs, engages in sexual intercourse with sleeping women. Many now believe that reports of incubi in fact describe incidents of sleep paralysis—a temporary state between sleeping and waking characterized by a brief immobility of the body and often accompanied by visual or auditory hallucinations. But it's difficult to discount the possibility that an incubus is an independent paranormal phenomenon, especially after you've spent a night alone at Bellaire House. Several cases of sexual assault by a malign spirit have occurred in the house. The entity responsible for these acts appears to have a preference for young blonde women, although these phantom assaults have been reported by men as well.

Bellaire House is available to rent for short stays—an option that frequently draws paranormal enthusiasts looking to spend a weekend in a genuine haunted house. But the house draws guests other than authentic investigators as well. One of the things I've learned as its owner is that some people prefer a haunted house to a motel. Once we even had a group who visited the house to film a show about ghost sex! I checked them in and left. But we have learned always to bleach the bedding and use rubber covers on all of the mattresses. After all, when visiting a haunted house, the maxim "safety first" doesn't refer just to the paranormal!

On one memorable occasion, a group of guests booked the house for a weekend stay. I have to admit that this particular group—three men in their sixties who claimed to own a "nightclub" and two beautiful young women in their twenties—gave me a sketchy feeling from the start. I got a very clear feeling that they hadn't come to the house just to investigate the paranormal. They had stayed with us before and always left empty cases of beer on the back porch, even though our website clearly warns against drinking or doing recreational drugs on the premises. In fact, I strongly advise everyone to leave their flasks and their "witch weed" at home when visiting haunted locations.

When I returned to see the group off at the end of the weekend, one of the young women (a blonde) told me that she had been sexually assaulted by an entity during their stay. She claimed that she was sleeping alone in her room when she felt something invisible penetrate her. She described being pinned down by this invisible force, which then proceeded to have sex with her. She didn't appear to be upset by the experience; she just wanted to know if it had ever happened to anyone else at Bellaire House. It had.

We know that there is a malign entity present in the house that controls the other spirits who reside there. We also know that it likes to hurt people and animals. And it doesn't stop there. This entity is very possessive and extremely negative. It appears to use sexual assault to assert its power over people, and as a way to leave its mark on them. In my research into the house and its paranormal activities, I found that those sleeping in the house are the ones most vulnerable to this entity. It creeps into their rooms at night in order to surprise and frighten them. When people are woken up in surprise, they often manifest fear, a strong energy on which this entity preys. Fear makes it stronger.

About a year before this particular woman reported this assault, we had hosted a Women in Paranormal event at the house. The event drew women from all over the country, many of whom had traveled great distances to stay at the house. A husband-and-wife team led the investigations, which got off to a very successful start, connecting with several of the house's spirits in the Séance Room. When it was time for the guests to retire to their rooms for the night, I left. Even though I own the house, I make it my practice never to spend the night there during scheduled events. I just don't feel comfortable sleeping in that house.

That night, a couple named Kristin and Bill were staying in the Emily Davis Room, a beautiful space with hardwood floors and a fireplace. Many guests request this room, because child spirits are often seen as less threatening. Many don't believe that the ghosts of children will do them harm, so they seem to feel more comfortable in Emily's room.

When I arrived back at Bellaire House in the afternoon of the next day, Kristin pulled me aside and said she needed to talk to me. I am skilled at reading the energy of others and I could tell by hers that something was wrong. Her aura was dull, almost as if were cracked, and something was clearly not right in her energy. I could tell that something was really bothering her, and that she was trying to maintain her composure and push through whatever it was that she was going through. Kristin is normally a very positive and vibrant woman who radiates a lot of good vibes, so I knew something was off.

Kristin told me that, the night before, she had had a frightening experience while sleeping. In the middle of the night, she sensed that something or someone had rolled over toward her and started touching her sexually. She knew her husband was asleep beside her, so she thought that they were about to have sex. She said her eyes were closed and that she could feel her husband's energy beside her. After a while, she opened her eyes to find that her husband was no longer in the room. She assumed he had gone to make coffee for them both, so she went downstairs to help him. When she found him in the kitchen doing dishes, she walked up behind him to hug him and commented on their recent intimacy. When Bill turned around and told her he had been downstairs for hours, her heart and stomach both dropped. It didn't make sense to her at all. She was absolutely certain that she had just had sex with her husband, but he had been nowhere near the bedroom for hours!

We now know that this malign entity likes to draw people into the Emily Davis Room in order to exploit and absorb their energy and become stronger. It uses sexual assault as a means to frighten them so it can feed on their fear and gain strength from it.

In the summer of 2019, eight guests stayed at Bellaire House for a week to make a film for a reality television show. During their stay, one blonde female guest reported to me that she was sexually assaulted by an entity. She claimed that, as she lay in bed, she had felt hands moving up her legs, and that these hands had also touched her chest. Then she felt something penetrate her. One of the male guests also reported that something had sexually assaulted him in the Edwin Heatherington Room. He was asleep after a long night of investigating when he was awakened by the door swinging open and a gust of cold air sweeping into the room. When he sat up to see what was going on, something pushed him backward with great force. He couldn't move for a few minutes. During this time of temporary paralysis, he saw a mass float across the room and begin to hover over him. He described what he felt as a powerful unknown entity having sex with him. Whatever it was, he claimed, felt as if it were uncontrollable.

We like to do an experiment with investigators who visit Bellaire House. We blindfold one investigator and ask him or her to wear a pair of headphones that are hooked up to a spirit box. Then another investigator asks his blindfolded colleague a series of questions. The blindfolded participant cannot hear these questions because of the headphones, but must instead answer by repeating what comes through from the spirit box.

When a friend of mine named Wes came to the house for a four-day afterlife data-collection session in February 2020, we conducted one of these experiments in the Jacob Heatherington Room. Wes was the blindfolded party. I asked him what spirits were among us and he responded with one name: "Jeff." I asked if that was the spirit's name and Wes said it wasn't. When I asked the spirit to tell Wes who he was, Wes simply repeated: "Jeff." This name struck a chord with me emotionally, as Jeff is the name of my son's biological father. But we also employed a groundskeeper named Jeff. I knew I had to stay calm, however, because it was possible that one of the house's more negative entities had invoked this name to get an emotional reaction out of me personally. I did not acknowledge these connections, but just sat for a few moments thinking quietly about what I should do next. Then I politely asked the spirit to tell us what it thought I should know and what it was trying to communicate. Wes responded: "Dog. Small dog. Black-and-white dog."

This was a very profound moment for me, because I knew that the spirit was referring to my deceased dog, Bella, who had been a black-and-white pit bull. While most people think of pit bulls as large dogs, Bella had always been on the small side. I had shared my life with Bella for eleven years. She had been with me when I moved into Bellaire House and had lived with me there during my initial stay. She had been my best friend and a truly special dog; there will never be another dog that could ever take her place.

At this point, Wes started to shift his weight back and forth. He looked uncomfortable, and his face twisted as if he were in emotional pain. I felt as if he were being shown visions of past events that had occurred either inside the house or on the land it sat on. Suddenly, Wes said: "Someone was sexually assaulted in this room. I can feel the fear. I can see the restraints." He took off the headphones and the blindfold and said: "This is too much for me." He excused himself for the rest of the session and left the room so that he could shake off the energy. When he came back, I told him that other investigators had reported sexual assaults while in the house. In tears, he said that he had felt the fear and knew that what had been reported by the investigators was real.

There are many different ways in which people can be haunted—by an actual ghost or by their own memories. As a psychologist, I understand that our brains sometimes try to keep us safe by blocking out traumatic memories. That trauma can reassert itself later in our lives in much the same way that a haunting can be viewed as the lingering impression of energy upon a place—perhaps physically stamped there by a death or a sexual assault. What we do not understand is why Wes was shown these specific visions that day in Bellaire House. There were inumerable other things that the spirit could have shown him. Perhaps this was a long-awaited confirmation that there really is a malicious entity within the house that preys on people while they sleep, that this is a real phenomenon that is not imagined or the result of sleep paralysis.

What I want readers to understand is that this malign spirit is very intelligent and very real. It can cause harm. Over the years, it's become clear to me that it wants to take investigators on a psychological rollercoaster ride in order to exhaust them mentally. This mental exhaustion leaves them vulnerable and wide open to actual physical harm. I have personally witnessed this type of activity several times in Bellaire House. It has thus become very important for me always to keep in mind that, when people witness this kind of paranormal phenomenon, it can be very dangerous to them emotionally, physically, and spiritually. We have to be able to separate our personal feelings or experiences from these phenomena in order to research them.

HELPFUL HINTS

If you find yourself spending the night at Bellaire House—or any haunted house, for that matter—I highly recommend that you do not stay alone. Have a trusted friend or companion sleep in the same room with you. Most of these ghostly assaults have been reported by individuals who were alone—or who thought they were alone—in a room at night. When investigating Bellaire House or other haunted locations, always remember that your safety is the most important thing. Take precautions to protect yourself. Wear crystals to ward off negative energy and malicious entities.

Avoid wearing black onyx, however, as it may affect you physically. It absorbs negative energy in a way that can wear down psychics and empaths, who are always hit harder by malign forces. Instead, you can "gift" a malicious spirit with black onyx, as it will repel their negative energy. If you visit Bellaire House and see pieces of black onyx placed around the house, please leave them alone. Do not pick them up or handle them. They are there to ward off malicious spirits and keep all who visit the house safe.

CHAPTER 11

Divide and Conquer

While I would dearly love to claim otherwise, the truth is that not every individual or team walks away from a stay at Bellaire House intact. The house is a manipulative, moody, and powerful force, and all the more dangerous for anyone who enters it already out of balance or harboring some form of spiritual attachment. Spirit attachments can make you feel tired, irritated, moody, and lethargic. Although the types of entities that attach themselves to investigators can typically be banished, in severe cases, some resist banishment by telling their targets that everything is perfectly normal and alright.

I've personally met quite a few people in the paranormal community who have very low-energy spirit attachments, and I know that it is possible for the spirits of Bellaire House to form these attachments with investigators. Edwin attached himself to Steven Huff after one of his visits, although he did eventually come back to the house. In this case, I personally feel that the attachment came from a spiritual connection between the two and from the fact that Edwin seems very fond of Steven.

Spirits try to attach themselves to a living body for a number of reasons. When we die, our spirits are supposed to leave our bodies to cross over into the afterlife, but sometimes unfinished business halts or hinders this process. Deprived of a physical body, these spirits may go in search of other living bodies in an attempt to complete this unfinished business. Some spirits have a difficult time coming to terms with death, so they try to attach themselves to living beings in order live through them. This is more common in the case of spirits who suffered a traumatic or sudden death. Alternatively, a spirit seeking an attachment may never have lived at all. There are many spirits that never existed in human form. These entities often try to take over the body and soul of a human in order to fulfill some kind of dark or negative act. This can be very dangerous and these entities may even intend to inflict harm or death on their chosen targets.

Energetic attachments like these are not to be confused with possession, however. They are simply fragments of emotional energy that can enter an individual's personal energy field or aura. Possession, on the other hand, involves a spirit actually entering and controlling a body. This can happen in two ways: through external possession, in which a spirit attaches itself to a body, usually via the back, and through internal possession, in which a spirit steps inside a soul body in order to compete with it for dominion. Internal possession is the kind most commonly portrayed in horror movies.

Possession can be extremely dangerous. Symptoms include, but are not limited to, abrupt personality or character changes, unexplained anger, and sudden outbursts of rage. Sometimes victims' eyes may appear lifeless or dull in color. Those possessed often lose their appetite or their need for sleep.

One paranormal team that I'd known for two years were frequent visitors to Bellaire House. They had spent several weekends there without any major harmful incidents. They were a pleasant group, not prone to drama or in-fighting, so I was happy to host them when they returned for another investigation. Little did any of us know that this would be their last investigation as a team. They checked in for a five-day lockdown—five straight days and nights locked inside the house with its spirits. When they arrived, friendly and personable as always, none of them had recently suffered a significant life-altering event of the kind that might trigger negativity and they were all seemingly free of spirit attachment. In fact, nothing seemed out of place. But at the end of those five days, they left the house loathing each other.

The house separated them, playing divide and conquer and turning them against each other. When I received a phone call from the team leader asking me to come and lend a hand, I found that the team had pushed all the couches together in the living room. They refused to go upstairs out of fear. Apparently, the house was "off the chain" that week, putting forth energy so strong that it was uncontrollable. As you already know, one of our firm rules at Bellaire House is that we have to step away when this happens. But this team really wanted to push through and stay for all five days. So, reluctantly, I allowed them to continue.

Another very important rule at Bellaire House is that we never provoke the spirits. Behaving in provocative or offensive ways in order to elicit an otherworldly response is strictly forbidden. But during this five-day lockdown, one of the team members broke this rule. He made a connection with a servant in the basement and called that servant a slave—something that is forbidden in the house. This is probably what started all the trouble. The situation then spiraled out of control, like one domino knocking down all the others in a chain of paranormal events.

The offending investigator kept trying to provoke this servant spirit into communication. He asked inappropriate questions and even went as far as to play slave spirituals to elicit a reaction. Well, he got one. He was scratched on his neck, on his back, and all the way down his ribcage. But that didn't stop him. As the days went on, he began instigating drama with his teammates. In the two years I had known him, I had never seen this man behave in this way. Because it was so out of character, it made me wonder if something inside the house had overwhelmed him. He was acting emotionally unbalanced, bragging about being financially well-off to people who knew that he wasn't, while simultaneously running up several thousand dollars of charges on a fellow investigator's credit card. His behavior fractured the team. They had walked in the best of friends and, within just a few days, the house had them screaming at each other. One investigator couldn't get out of bed for two days because he felt so completely drained. But the worst was yet to come.

At one point, I went for a walk with one of the female team members so she could clear herself of the negativity the house was inflicting on the team. As we walked, she asked me to tell her about fallen angels. She said that she always felt different inside Bellaire House, as if she were in the midst of a battle between good and evil—and she couldn't tell which side she was on. I told her that, according to Christian doctrine, God, in His infinite power, created a multitude of angels—so many of them that their number was incalculable. These angels, who were God's pure messengers, were subjected to a trial of obedience and humility before being granted permission to enter heaven. But Satan, who was the most beautiful of all the angels, rebelled at the idea of having to prove himself. When other angels followed his lead and rebelled as well, they fell from God's grace. Expelled from heaven for their sin of pride and disobedience, they descended to earth as demons. When Father Candido Amantini, a renowned priest and exorcist, once asked a demon how many there were like him, the demon responded: "We are so many that, if we were visible, we would obscure the sun."

As we returned to the house, I explained that the most important thing to realize in a spiritual battle is that you cannot back down and you cannot let your emotions get the best of you. There are times when malign entities can make us feel great sadness. They may show us visions in an attempt to influence us, or even show us personal experiences we've endured in the past to try to wear us down. I stressed how important it was to control these emotions. When we don't, these entities can drain us psychologically and even affect us physically. I warned the woman that these spiritual battles could have an adverse effect on her personal life, even outside of the battle—that her life might become abruptly negative and her behavior abnormal. She was silent for a moment and then said: "Do you mean the way my team member has been behaving?"

And then it suddenly hit me what was happening. We had been talking for hours, but at no point had the woman suggested that her team member might be suffering from a case of possession. Instead, she had led me in circles, continually deflecting my conclusions and drawing more and more information from me. Then I realized that she had been in the house just as long as everyone else, and that she was probably affected as well. Something malign was using her as a host! I jumped back in alarm as she turned to look at me and saw something different about her eyes as she stared at me. I remembered something that Kat Lang had once told me about victims of possession: "They don't blink, Kris. They won't."

And this woman didn't blink at all. She began speaking, referring to personal things she couldn't possibly have known about me. She said my father's name and my great-grandmother's name; she called out the name of my deceased cat. I was in a panic. Dealing with a malicious entity is stressful at the best of times, and this one had snuck up on me. I was afraid, and I knew that it knew that. I started to calm my breathing so I could control my mind. I knew that I had no choice but to disregard the personal attacks being thrown at me. The entity was using the names of my deceased loved ones to weigh me down and make me emotional, trying to break me. But this wasn't the first time Bellaire House had attacked me. After a minute, I had myself under control enough so that I could speak.

"I know you're in there," I said, speaking directly to the woman and ignoring the entity. "I know something has you."

"F*** you, Kristin!" the entity said. "F*** your dog Bella too! F*** you, f*** you, f*** you!" But no matter what it said to me, I couldn't turn my back on this woman. She was my friend, my guest, and a mother. I knew I had to look out for her.

Then I realized that I had a bottle of water in my hand and that there was kosher salt on the table beside me. Emboldened, I said: "You have no power here because I know what you are. And you don't have control over this woman because she knows what you are. I command you to leave her now!"

"You're pathetic," the entity said, as it laughed at me.

I picked up the kosher salt and flung down a handful. A smell like sulfur rose into the air just as two other members of the investigation team entered, completely unaware of what had just transpired. As they walked into the room, however, I could tell that they knew something was deeply wrong with their friend. When they asked me if I needed any help, I told them to start praying and that, whatever happened, not to stop. I needed them with me, to stand their ground and not back down.

The woman didn't make any move to rise. She just sat there, staring directly at me. That told me that it was I that the entity really wanted. I grabbed some holy water that was nearby in the kitchen and combined it with the kosher salt in my water bottle. Then I told one of the investigators to call Kat Lang.

"Kat is dead," the entity said. "I killed her. She won't answer!"

This was almost too much for me and I very nearly lost my cool. "Try again!" I cried. "I'm not backing down. You have thirty seconds to get out of Edwin and Lyde's house or I'll drench you with this holy water!" I used their names deliberately to call their spirits into the room. The other team members looked paralyzed, but they continued to pray.

Then the energy finally shifted and I felt Edwin's presence. Emboldened by this, I threw the whole bottle of holy water on the possessed woman. She began to scream as if I had thrown acid on her, even though there was nothing in the bottle but salt water. We all stood back as the lights in the house began to flicker. We heard a huge banging noise, as if something very heavy had fallen over, and the windows began to shake as if the wind had picked up. It was as if the sky had suddenly been obscured by clouds; although still daylight outside, darkness was falling inside the house. The woman had turned pale, her face taking on a gray cast as if she were about to be sick. She slouched down in her seat as if she had lost control of her body, and one of her fellow investigators ran over to support her. Panic gripped me. I had been through so many experiences in Bellaire House, but that didn't make something this sudden any easier to live through. I did the only thing I could think of in that moment—I prayed.

As quickly as the storm had begun, it stopped. The pressure was gone and the energy inside the house dropped drastically. In the ensuing silence, I felt that, if I opened the door to the world outside, it would appear as a technicolor wonderland. I felt that, if I flung open the windows, I would see my very own Land of Oz.

The woman came back to us after that. I drew her a salt bath to cleanse her of any remaining malicious influence and sat with her in the bathroom as she lay in the tub. She slept through the night. But the rest of us were very shaken, so no one else slept and we hardly even spoke to each other. We were all depleted, just trying to wrap our heads around what we'd experienced. The provocative team member's behavior improved visibly as the house's hold on him loosened, and his normal personality reasserted itself. If the others hadn't been with me to confirm the experience, I might have thought that I'd gone completely delusional. I wondered how I could possibly explain this experience, or if anyone would believe me if I tried. The house had shocked me to the core that day and the weight of that experience still lies heavy on my mind today.

It's hard to describe just how deeply Bellaire House can sink its hooks into a person's inner mind, penetrating the normal barriers of the ego and going deep down into the subconscious mind. This influence opens us up to our most deeply buried thoughts and fears, inducing a feedback loop of fear and paranoia. Experienced investigators have to learn to avoid this, as the resulting mental state can render them useless for the purposes of paranormal data collection. Seeing the affected investigator revert back to his old self gave me some sense of relief. The team all seemed happy and we went out to dinner together to celebrate the end of the lockdown. Some even went into town to get tattoos of the house and its ghosts. Although everything seemed bright and sunny, however, the storm had not yet passed. The team may have left the house, but its influence still lingered with them.

Two weeks after they left Bellaire House, the team disbanded. Eight months after the lockdown, one member's personal relationship had deteriorated to the point that she almost got a divorce, while another lost her home in a fire. The investigator who had instigated all the trouble by provoking the spirit of the servant in the basement left his family; none of us have heard from him since.

HELPFUL HINTS

Though far less severe than possession, spirit attachment is something that you can pick up anywhere—even in the most mundane places, like at the grocery store or perhaps sitting in a restaurant. You can also pick up attachments from the people around you. If you're in the presence of someone who is in a foul mood and you feel your own spirits begin to sag, there may be something more to it than just a sour companion. On some basic level, we're all attuned to each other's energy. Think of negative energy as a parasite that can latch on to your own energy, sucking away at it. We become especially susceptible to these attachments when we are feeling vulnerable or lacking in spiritual protection. They can make us feel tired, irritated, moody, and lethargic when we are normally energetic and upbeat.

The intensity of these feelings can depend on the degree of the attachment. You can get rid of lesser attachments by using the power of conscious positive thinking or by performing a spiritual cleansing. Crystals like smoky quartz and black onyx repel negative energies and entities, so wear them to protect yourself. Sage and essential oils of lime and lavender can also help strengthen your protection from negative attachments, as does prayer, incense, and religious amulets. However you choose to protect yourself, it is vital to build a strong shield to ward off these energies, especially if you work or live in a highly emotional environment.

CHAPTER 12

What Lies Below

Every haunted house needs a haunted basement and Bellaire House does not disappoint. When you walk through the kitchen into the hallway and look to your right, you see the steps that lead down into the depths of the house. If you look up, you can see the first floor's wood flooring through the ceiling. The basement is divided into two sections: one contains the furnace, while the other contains a wall with a bricked-up doorway that once led through a secret passage to the tunnels that run underneath the house. Although this passageway is no longer accessible, the wall, which is now painted green, still contains an extremely active portal.

In fact, the basement is now one of the house's most active rooms, perhaps because of its close proximity to the underground world of Bellaire, which used to be a coal-mining town as well as a stop on the Underground Railway. Guests and paranormal investigators alike have felt phantom touches, heard strange whispers, and even seen the apparition of a large ghostly snake there. The basement is, indeed, home to a bevy of spirits, notably former servants of the house, Native Americans, and various earthbound entities. While many of these have made their presence known in the basement, none have ever identified themselves by name.

It's perhaps no surprise that the Bellaire House basement exhibits such a high level of paranormal activity, since there is a long and fascinating underground history related to both the house and the town. One of Jacob Heatherington's former coal mines, still accessible from Belmont Street, is located only 300 feet from the house. There are Native American burial caves located behind the house, and Native American spirits have been known to manifest within the basement. One previous code enforcer told me that there were tunnels running everywhere underneath the town in addition to those that were part of the coal mines. One of these runs directly beneath Bellaire House and is likely where the bricked-up passageway used to lead.

In one part of the basement, there is a built-in cabinet and some old shelves, underneath which is an old coal chute where we captured some very exciting afterlife data. The spirit, which could see us, told us that we were "small." When I asked if there were dogs and cats in the afterlife, a voice said: "My dog is here with me."

Visitors have reported seeing a ghostly snake in the basement, most often on the floor by the back wall, right by the walled-up secret passageway. It is shadowy in appearance and has been described as a mixture of smoke and vapor. Witnesses have also said that the snake appears to give off heat, like steam rising from a car engine on a cold morning. The snake appears to be some form of spirit, perhaps even a fire elemental manifesting in the form of a serpent. While some have found the spirit snake creepy, I find it fascinating. To me, it is a symbol of protection that can ward against evil forces. I see it as a spirit guide from Apollo, with both reptilian and masculine energies that protect the house's human visitors from its unearthly inhabitants.

Often when we are setting up our equipment, the house's energy suddenly shifts to the place in the basement where the shadow snake has most often been seen. I think it's very possible that the snake is protecting us from something even darker. I once had a dream in which the house showed me a baby alligator that lived underneath the left side of the front porch. It was clear in the dream that the alligator was protecting the house. I view the basement's spirit snake in much the same way; as a benevolent spiritual protector. If you visit the Bellaire House basement, be sure to keep an eye open for something slithering in the dark as you descend the stairs.

One visiting paranormal investigator picked up on an entity in the basement that she thought lived behind the water heater. Describing her encounter with it, she said she felt as if it had spent some time touching the top of her head. Her husband also reported that he felt as if he were being touched by this entity. They described it as seeming "curious, but cautious," but without any sort of malevolent intent. It is not uncommon while in the basement to experience these phantom touches. When Bishop Long and I were filming there, we both felt something touch the backs of our necks. In our case, it felt as if whatever touched us had come from the back of the basement.

Allison has also been touched while in the basement. Neither Allison nor I enjoy spending a lot of time there; there's just something about its energy that gives us both the feeling that we would do best to steer clear. For the purposes of paranormal investigation, however, we occasionally have to venture down into the house's depths. More than once while setting up cameras, Allison has felt otherworldly presences, heard scuffling, or been touched by phantom hands. She and I have both heard tapping in the basement that we can't explain and heard whispers that we can't understand. Allison described the touches she experienced there as being very light taps, like pokes, on her shoulders, her upper arms, and her shoulder blades—almost as if something or someone were trying to get her attention.

Not all experiences in the basement are positive, harmless touches, however. The basement, like the rest of the house, has also seen its share of violent encounters. One entity always creeps up from below during séances. And the portal in the basement, like the rest of the portals in the house, may be responsible for a large amount of the house's paranormal activity. When I sought paranormal investigator Joe Estes's expertise in locating all of the portals in the house, we tackled the one in the basement together. We threw candle wax onto it and, to my astonishment, the image of someone who had once lived in the house appeared in the spot where the wax landed. This person had been a very negative force both inside the house and in my personal life. He'd invoked and worshiped very negative energies while he lived in the house and personally caused me harm. I hadn't seen him for quite some time. But when his face appeared to me, it almost looked as if he were staring back at us from the portal, as if he had been watching the entire time. According to Joe, the bricked-up passageway is the only portal in the basement—but it's one hell of a portal.

Another investigator, Jim Backus, has also had powerful paranormal experiences in the Bellaire House basement. When a group of us stayed in the house to film a program for television, Jim elected to sleep there on an air mattress. One night, he felt as if someone were standing over him, but there was no one there. Jim described it as a dark mass that seemed to distort the natural sounds of the night. The next night, as he lay in bed, he felt as if someone suddenly stepped onto the air mattress; he even heard the plastic squeak. He rolled a little bit and then heard shuffling. Both of these sensations were brief, but they came with a wave of heaviness and an awareness of the presence of another being—like when you can sense without looking that there is someone, or something, standing behind you.

As this entity backed into the furnace area, it appeared to Jim to be about the size of a person—although he never saw a human shape, just a mass of energy that felt heavy with intent. He felt the bed being pressed down under the weight of something and then heard shuffling sounds as it retreated toward the furnace. After that, Jim left the basement and slept upstairs for the next few nights. When he shared these experiences with me, he told me that, if he weren't experienced with the paranormal and used to these kinds of energies, he probably wouldn't have been able to stay in the basement as long as he had.

One incident that involved the basement is very memorable to me, in no small part because, even by my standards, it was incredibly bizarre. After the demonology seminar that Bishop Long conducted at Bellaire House, I received a phone call from a woman who refused to give her name. She claimed to be a psychic and told me that she had experienced a terrifying premonition regarding the house. In this premonition, a woman arrived at the house bringing with her a young autistic boy who was in her care. She sensed that the child was in incredible peril and warned me that the situation would become extremely dangerous if I reopened the house to the public. She was extremely emotional during the phone call, crying and begging me not to reopen the house.

Something about the woman's tone and her desperation struck a chord with me, and I wondered if she might actually be a psychic who had experienced a terrifying vision of the future. After all, I had had my own terrifying experiences in the house and was still on edge about what the future might bring if I reopened it. I wasn't ready to discount any possibilities. I called Kat Lang and Bishop Long for advice, but they reassured me that we had enough resources to handle the spirits in the house and that there was no reason not to proceed with the grand reopening and the planned afterlife studies. Reassured, I tried to put the strange phone call out of my mind, writing it off as just another one of those bizarre experiences that came almost daily with ownership of the house.

I had almost entirely forgotten about the phone call when, a few weeks later, I received an email from a woman in California inquiring about renting the house. She told me that she had a friend who worked for HBO and that she wanted to document her experiences for them. This seemed like a great opportunity, so we agreed that she should fly in to see the house. Daniel and I greeted her and offered to give her a tour. As we showed her around, she told us that she had a young autistic son. Instantly, I remembered the psychic who had begged me not to turn the house into an afterlife research center. I tried to tell myself it was just a coincidence, but things truly took a turn for the bizarre when Daniel and I took the woman into the basement. It was there, underground, that she confided to me that she had a connection to Lilith, mother of all demons. Suddenly, the lightbulb above us exploded and glass went flying everywhere, shards raining down on our heads as we ducked and covered our faces. It was like a warning from the house not to get involved with the woman from California. I never heard from her again after that incident.

The exploding lightbulb is far from the only violent incident that has taken place in the Bellaire House basement. A woman named Kellyann once sent me an email in which she told me that her wife, Rett, had stayed in the house frequently during her childhood and that they wanted to revisit. When they arrived, it took a while for Rett to feel comfortable setting foot inside the house. It was clear to me that she had experienced something otherworldly there. She revealed to me that, as a child, she had had many paranormal experiences in the house that had changed her perception of both life and the afterlife forever. Some of the activity Rett described is truly disturbing. She told me that when she slept over at the house, which at the time was the home of her best friend, she always stayed in the bedroom at the end of the hall—the Edwin Heatherington Room, which has been the site of much recorded paranormal activity.

Rett recalled that, one night when she was asleep, she suddenly awoke to find that she was floating above the bed, as if she had been levitated. She had a full and vivid view of the room while this was going on and could see her friend sleeping in the corner. She couldn't explain how she started to levitate or what entity had lifted her up. She also recalled a time when she was locked in the bathroom for hours by an unseen force. She cried and screamed for help, but it seemed that no one else in the house could hear her. She felt as if she had been alone in the room for hours when she suddenly heard the lock click and, ever so slowly, the door appeared to open on its own. Rett believed that an entity had kept her in there against her will, but she couldn't understand why. On another occasion, she brought her baby nephew with her to meet her friend's family. As they sat in the dining room with the baby in his carrier, she saw the carrier—baby and all—suddenly levitate clear off the ground! The whole family witnessed this incident, but, since they were a very strict Catholic family, they refused to acknowledge any of the paranormal activity that happened in the house.

Rett came back to the house the following year for one of our public paranormal investigations. Her wife loved everything paranormal and Rett wanted to please her by coming with her. The investigation went well and, toward the middle of the night, Rett felt confident enough to go with a group into the basement. I told her that I would be upstairs in Command Central and that she should let me know if she felt uncomfortable. I said that Mike Simpson, who was leading the basement group, would bring her back upstairs. Just minutes into the basement session, the night's activity skyrocketed. Mike reported afterward that strange growling sounds began to emanate from the equipment almost as soon as the session started. The energy in the basement shifted dramatically and became dark. Mike described it as feeling like a cold rain. He later told me that he had never seen energy shift so fast as when the entity in the basement turned on Rett.

Upstairs in Command Central, everything looked normal to me—right up until Rett began to scream. Mike quickly got her upstairs, where we discovered that something in the basement had scratched her badly. She had three long, deep scratches on her lower back and three on her neck. We were all shaken by the violent activity that had been aimed at her. She stayed with me for the rest of the night, and I made sure to cleanse her with kosher salt and give her a protection bag filled with iron nails and wolf hair. I also gave her my crystal pendant to wear around her neck for additional protection. I was worried about residual energy following her and affecting her psychologically, so I made her promise to stay in touch with me.

These days, I rarely go into the basement myself. The stairs are steep and difficult to navigate, and I try to avoid them given the high level of unpredictable activity that occurs below. I've been pushed down the second story stairs before and I have no wish to repeat the experience with the basement steps. The house has banged me up pretty badly over the years and, personally, I have had enough. Today, most of the basement activity is reported to me by other paranormal investigators or by guests.

HELPFUL HINTS

You can use this spell to dissipate the negativity energy in the Bellaire House basement or at any other haunted site. It involves burying an object in the ground, in much the same way that a basement is beneath the ground. Take a bowl of spring water mixed with kosher salt and place it at the very center of the location in question, then add silver to it—coins or jewelry will do. The negative entities in the house will be drawn to the silver and, when they see their reflection in the bowl, they will become trapped in the water. Once the water in the bowl evaporates and the salt that remains looks white and crusty, take the bowl to the northern-most part of the property and bury it. The best place to bury a spell bowl like this is under a willow tree.

CHAPTER 13

The Dreaming House

Bellaire House is much more than "just" a haunted house: it holds the power of prophecy and has the ability to predict the future and communicate it to those within its walls. The house does contain the spirits of psychics, like Edwin Heatherington, who continues to do work as a medium even after his death. But the house has also shown time and time again that it can make predictions independently. It seems to have an awareness of the world outside of its walls, and can apparently sense the outside lives of those who venture inside to investigate.

To visualize the energy inside Bellaire House, close your eyes and imagine the planet Saturn, with its orbiting rings. Those circling cosmic dust storms are like the psychic energies within the house, which are often sensed as a powerful gust of wind. These energies circle within themselves, and then move into visiting psychics, healers, empaths, and light-workers. The energy downloads and uploads itself, treating both humans and spirits like computers whose data can be accessed and decoded. This can have a very disorienting effect on people. In the house, you may feel like the human embodiment of a fun-house mirror reflection, tilted this way and that. The house can even turn itself into an *ouroboros,* a snake eating its own tail, feeding off the same forces that it feeds to energy-sensitive visitors, creating an energy loop.

I have witnessed and been told about many occasions on which the house has made accurate predictions about personal aspects of people's lives. More than once, an investigator has been told to leave the premises and return home to prevent a disaster. Some of these stories are very distributing, even to me. Despite everything else the house has put me through, however, I've learned to trust it when it makes these kinds of predictions. Bellaire House is unpredictable. It can feel like a television set whose channels are constantly changing. But I've learned that, if a house spirit says "attic," then you go to the attic. If it says "danger, go home," then you go home. When the spirits of the house make their feelings—and their predictions—known to you, you are wise to listen.

Bellaire House reached its darkest level in 2008 and 2009. Indeed, the house itself became unlivable during this period. Nothing would have induced me to set foot back inside it. And yet, despite the terrifying darkness that settled over the house, the intelligence of the spirits who communicated with us was unbelievable and otherwordly. Many of these were protective spirits who foretold upcoming danger. They often warned if someone was being manipulated spiritually or was potentially at risk of being harmed by a malign entity within the house, and they cautioned those whose loved ones might be in danger or subject to harm.

There was one darker entity, however, who seemed to have influence even outside the house. And it tried in every way it could to keep us from identifying it as just what it was—a malevolent force. Indeed, we haven't yet been able to pin down exactly what this entity is or how it came to be in the house. But I do know, from hard experience, the awful and terrifying harm that it can inflict upon myself and others.

At the time, I had not been inside Bellaire House for over a year and I was still shaken from the trauma I had experienced there. In fact, it took me years to be able to walk back inside and feel physiologically safe. Part of my process of recovery was to learn about the house and understand the entities that reside there.

I wasn't satisfied just knowing that the house was haunted. I wanted to discover the cause, to classify it and explore it. So I asked Mike McCallister to help me. But Mike was not immune to the house's incredible level of activity either. The malign entity taunted him, repeating the names of his wife and children. On his drive home after one session, the car radio started emitting static and the entity's voice came over the airwaves, saying his name over and over as he drove away from the house.

Once, while Mike was investigating on the second floor of the house, he heard the voice of Lyde, who has a very particular presence within the house—it feels as if she's been there for all eternity.

"Michael, go home," she said. "Danger at home."

When Mike returned home, he discovered that one of his children had been terribly hurt. He told me that he felt that Lyde had warned him, showing a level of concern and benevolence that neither of us expected to find in the house. After all, I had been violently assaulted there and one entity had told Mike that it was going to kill me! Another investigator reported receiving a relative's name while inside the house. No matter what she asked, this name came back to her again and again. Before long, she received a phone call telling her to come home at once; that relative was ill.

Moreover, the reach of the house extends beyond simply knowing of events that are happening outside its walls; it seems that it can influence physical objects as well. One frequent phenomenon involves the stopping or stalling of cars. In 2009, an investigator reported that his car broke down at exactly the same mile marker every time he headed for the house. I didn't think very much of it at the time; it was unusual, but we've all experienced odd car trouble at some point. In 2017, however, the phenomenon began to repeat itself with a different investigator. Soon, two more investigators reported that their cars broke down at the exact same spot. This raised a lot of questions, and we began to wonder whether this might be a paranormal hotspot in its own right, unrelated to Bellaire House.

If this were so, however, why weren't other breakdowns reported among those who were not Bellaire House investigators? Because I personally know that the forces inside the house have stalled my car before—for example, the night when the house prevented me from leaving by stalling my car in the driveway, it seemed likely to me that these breakdowns were caused directly by the house. But if that were the case, why did some investigators experience car trouble and not others? Was the house attempting to prevent only certain people from reaching its doors? And if so, why? Perhaps for their own protection? I don't know. All I know is that, if you're driving to Bellaire House and you break down on Highway 70 East, beware. The house may be trying to tell you something.

On one occasion, a group of strangers showed up at the house at two in the morning, claiming that they had bought tickets to an event that had already ended. They demanded to be let in to investigate, but couldn't show us proof that they had even bought tickets to the event. Eventually, we had to call the police, who convinced the belligerent strangers to leave. The officers who responded to the call then expressed curiosity about the house and what we were doing there. They'd heard rumors about our paranormal investigations and had plenty of questions for us. Even though it was late, we were grateful for their help with the strangers, so we invited them in and asked if they wanted to participate in a paranormal investigation session. We used Steven Huff's portal to amplify and enhance any spiritual communication that might come through. Allison showed the officers how to use the device, instructing one to place a hand on the copper wire to make a spiritual connection and the other hand on a quartz crystal, then prompted him to ask a question.

"What's my son's name?" asked the officer.

A voice came through the box: "Able." The officer physically recoiled, jumping back, then walked around the room quietly repeating: "Oh my God, oh my God." We waited for him to say something else, or perhaps for more spirit communication to come through the box. Finally, when the officer had calmed down a little, Allison asked if his son's name was, in fact, Able.

"Yes," he replied, adding that his son had passed away at a young age.

The officers stayed with us for about an hour. We gave them a full tour of the house and shared our own experiences with them. Despite the night's rough start, it ended up being a great experience, and I was gratified that we were able to help the officer connect with his deceased son. To this day, I wonder if those belligerent ticket holders were actually sent by the house spirits as a way of bringing those police officers to us.

Many investigators have reported that they have had accurate dreams of the interior of Bellaire House and its ghosts before they ever physically set foot inside it. Daniel, my husband, dreamed of the house in 2000, years before he ever laid eyes on it. "I remember being there," he claims, "but I was never there." This dream wasn't like his normal dreams, he recalls, but more like a confirmation for him, a feeling of awareness that he was on a path. In the dream, he was cooking in the kitchen before walking from there into the dining room. We were talking about music. He wasn't able to see me in the dream, although he could hear my voice. This was all very clear in his mind's eye.

Fast forward to 2013, when Daniel was in the house with me. One night, he was cooking in the kitchen. As he started to serve the food, he became aware that his actions were following the exact pattern of his earlier dream—like rewinding and watching a movie of himself or seeing his reflection in a different time dimension. As he turned the corner with the dinner plates balanced on his hands, he felt cold chills run through his body as he took the exact same steps he had dreamed thirteen years before. And as the dream repeated itself in real life, he realized that we *were* talking about music and that, now, he could see me. Daniel has also dreamed of other people before they arrived at Bellaire House. He dreamed of meeting Mike Simpson and shaking his hand in the living room six years before they ever met in the physical world. And, in fact, when they did meet, the first thing Mike did was shake Daniel's hand in the living room.

This feeling of *déjà vu*, the sense of having already lived through a present situation, is pervasive at Bellaire House, where time seems to flow differently. Imagine two record players playing the exact same song at the exact same time, but one song is pitched lower than the other, its sound cloudy, faint, and distant. It's a multidimensional experience, a time slip, the colliding of a past and present life, of dreaming and reality. The attic, in particular, seems to be a hotspot for this kind of experience, as well as for those who walk the house in their dreams. Several investigators have reported, after their first trip to the attic, that they had seen it before, either in dreams or in prophecy, almost like an out-of-body experience. It seems that Bellaire House makes all things possible.

When we dream, we are in a relaxed state of mind. Our physical bodies are at peace. This is one of the reasons why we are most open to spirit travel during sleep; our spirits can leave our physical forms and travel to locations where we may never have been in our waking lives, leaving us with knowledge and memories of these places. Of course, we can't rule out the possibility that, when visiting a famous location, we may previously have absorbed knowledge about it through photographs or literature and that these subconscious memories can account for a sense of *déjà vu*. It would be easy for images of the Eiffel Tower or the Statue of Liberty to imprint themselves on our minds, leading us to feel as if we've already been there by the time we see them in person. But this is perhaps less true for an ordinary-looking house in Belmont County, Ohio, where, if you look at the windows from the outside for too long, you wonder if it's just your imagination, or if something is actually moving behind them.

HELPFUL HINTS

It is difficult to offer advice for dealing with Bellaire House in dreams, because it is the house itself and the spirits inside it that decide whether or not to show themselves to select guests before they ever visit. Some even continue to have nightmares after they leave the house. There is no way to control this pre- or post-visit dreaming and I have no convenient spell to protect against it. This phenonmenon is as uncontrollable as the house itself. But there are ways that you can influence these dreams. There are also ways you can protect yourself while you dream and ways you can guard against nightmares.

For instance, you can petition Archangel Michael to bring you a specific dream. First, cleanse and purify yourself using whatever methods you prefer. My go-to method is to draw a bath and mix kosher salt into the water. After you are cleansed, light an oil lamp. Speak into the lamplight and focus on it until it burns out. As you watch, repeat this incantation: "Lamp, light the way to Archangel Michael. If my petition is appropriate, show me water and a grave. If not, show me water and a stone." You must say this just as the lamp goes out. Then, without saying another word, go to sleep and dream.

For extra protection while dreaming and to guard against nightmares, place a crystal on a clean white handkerchief along with some dream herbs like chamomile, lavender, or linden flowers. Tie the corners of the handkerchief together with a blue silk ribbon to make a sachet. Do not sew it; you will want to remove the crystal periodically to cleanse it, especially in the aftermath of a bad nightmare. Sleep with this sachet under your pillow and take it apart to cleanse it as needed.

CHAPTER 14

Healing Waters

Bellaire House has been the site of so much trauma, harm, and terror. But it has also been the site of miraculous healing, both spiritual and physical. The house's moods are mercurial; the population of ghosts, spirits, and entities found inside are varied and unpredictable. You can't come to Bellaire House expecting to know how things will go on any particular day; you can only protect yourself, and see what the house has in store for you.

We always book reservations for the house in groups or pairs. Given the house's history and nature, we don't want anyone to stay there completely alone, because we feel that it's unsafe to do so. One woman requested that she be allowed to stay in the house alone for a few days before being joined by her friends.

I refused and told her that it was against the house rules. If she wanted to come, she had to have someone stay with her. She tried to bargain with me, saying that she needed to get away to find some peace and tranquility, and that she felt very drawn to Bellaire House. Again I refused and told her that there were no exceptions to this rule. In the end, she agreed.

The woman was supposed to check in on a Friday and be joined by her friends a few hours later. That Wednesday afternoon, two days before she was supposed to arrive, she called me and said she was at the house and wanted to be let in. When I went to meet her, I found her alone and reiterated that she could not be in the house without a companion. She assured me that she would be fine, telling me that she had been to places that she referred to as "darker locations."

"We have all been to dark places," I replied, "but I still need to make sure you're safe."

It was then that I noticed that the woman's arms and legs were covered in open sores. She had visible wounds all over her body, but she didn't seem to be distressed by them at all. Considering her condition and her determination to stay in the house, I relented, telling her that I would open the house for her on the condition that I would also send around people who were familiar with the house's nature to check up on her from time to time. I arranged for Kat Lang to stay with her overnight. Reluctantly, she agreed.

The woman was very excited as I opened the house. She seemed to feel no trepidation or anxiety at all about being there. As we walked around, I told her a little about the house, and she decided that she would stay in the Edwin Heatherington Room. Before I left, I told her that our groundskeeper, Goat, would arrive shortly to sit with her until Kat came to stay the night. I gave her a copy of the waiver we require all guests to sign before staying overnight in the house and put the original signed copy in the hutch. As the owner of a haunted location, it's very important to me that I keep all waivers organized and on site while people are visiting. I also gave her my personal cell phone number in case of an emergency. Then I reminded her that no witchcraft or conjuring whatsoever was allowed. She agreed.

When it was time for me to leave, something kept me from going. I had an odd feeling in my gut that something was wrong and I hesitated, feeling reluctant to leave the woman alone in the house. But she had agreed to all of my stipulations and signed the required liability waiver, so there was not much more that I could do. Before I left, I told her that I would put her on the guest list for a lecture about the paranormal that I was giving that evening, thinking that it would be good for her to get out of the house for a few hours. It can be hard to tell how strongly the house's energy is affecting you while you're in the midst of it. After all, it always seems calmest in the eye of the storm. This would also give my friends time to arrive so she wouldn't be all alone. Satisfied that I had done all I could, I finally left.

Shortly afterward, the woman called me to tell me that she had taken a long bath to heal her wounds. I assumed at first that she meant her emotional wounds. She didn't. When I went to check on her later with Goat and my husband, she showed me her arms and legs, which, just a short while ago, had been covered in open sores. They appeared to be completely healed. I wouldn't have believed it if I hadn't seen it for myself. She claimed that the waters of the house had healed her, and that Lyde wanted her to stay—permanently. Lyde, she said, was the one who had healed her. I had to admit that it was pretty miraculous.

The woman stayed at Bellaire House for a few more days, wearing an odd Victorian stage costume both in the house and around town while running errands. She was quite vocal in her assertations that it was Lyde who had healed her, telling me this several times. She also said that she spent a lot of time recharging in the house's bath. Finally, when it came time for her to depart, she wouldn't. She claimed that Lyde wanted her to move in and gave no indication that she intended to leave. When Kat called to tell me this, Daniel and I decided to go to the house to resolve the issue. After we made it clear that she must leave, she spent some time upstairs talking to Lyde while Daniel and I waited on the first floor. When she brought her packed bags downstairs, there were tears in her eyes. As we saw her off, she told us that she loved Lyde and that she wanted to come back and spend more time with her. Despite these words, I haven't seen or heard from her since that day.

This was not the only healing to occur at Bellaire House. Another woman arrived there with the intention of connecting to the afterlife. Unbeknownst to us at the time, she suffered from a form of brain cancer, although she didn't say what type and I didn't press her for specifics. It was apparently very painful, however. During her stay at the house, she kept a jug filled with some type of herbal liquid in the refrigerator that she said helped her with the pain.

While we were in session, this woman said that she felt hands on her shoulders, and that she felt as if this touch were healing her. I hadn't known before then that she was ill; that information came out during the session. As I sat beside her, I developed a terrible headache that started on the left side of my head and then spread all over, although the pain remained the worst on the left. Once I had shared that I had a sharp pain in my head and that it was absolutely awful, the woman revealed to us that she suffered from brain cancer. It was as if the session had allowed me to feel her pain. A few weeks later, she contacted us to report that she had not felt any symptoms since the session. She wasn't fully healed; she was still ill and assured us that she continued to see her doctor. But her pain had subsided substantially and the effects seemed to be more than just a temporary remission. She believed that either Eliza or Lyde had healed her.

It would be useful to know for sure whether either Lyde or Eliza can truly heal people. We know that they are both the earthbound spirits of people who once lived in the house. Moreover, we know that Eliza suffered from depression during her lifetime. If her spirit has healing abilities, perhaps it comes from an empathy for the afflicted and for those in pain. Lyde lived a long life, allegedly dying of a heart attack in the house. Perhaps this prompts her spirit to want to ease the physical suffering of others. If Lyde and Eliza truly have the ability to heal wounds and soothe pain, it would be a fascinating development. It would be especially interesting to know if this healing power is something inherent in their spirits or if it is drawn from the intense metaphysical and supernatural power of the house itself. Could the house, in fact, either amplify or grant this ability? This is something that definitely needs to be researched in the future.

While Eliza and Lyde, along with their family member Edwin, are long-term otherworldly residents of Bellaire House, I suspect that they are not bound to it on a permanent basis and that they can travel outside of its walls. We sometimes receive very minimal communication from them when we ask them to speak with us during sessions, as if they are not entirely present. This is a marked change from when they are entirely present within the house, when we've been able to talk to them for up to two or three hours at a time. Yet sometimes it feels as if they've gone somewhere else. Perhaps they can leave Bellaire House on a temporary basis to help a loved one crossover, or perhaps they sometimes have one foot on earth and one foot in the afterlife.

The study of long-term earthbound spirits is of particular interest me; I want to know how and why they've stayed so long. Are they afraid of change? Is Bellaire House simply where they feel the most comfortable? Do they know they are spirits and just don't want to leave? On the other hand, can it be that they have no choice but to stay—that Bellaire House is such a beacon of metaphysical energy that it draws spirits to it and keeps them stuck there, like a powerful magnet drawing in iron filings?

Not all healings that have occurred in Bellaire House are strictly physical. Many people come to us hoping to find healing and solace in the affirmation of the existence of an afterlife; many come to communicate with their deceased loved ones. One girl named Marci came to us to make contact with her deceased father. She wanted to tell him how sorry she was that she hadn't been with him in the moment he transitioned. Through a spirit-box session, she asked Edwin to find her father in the afterlife and request that he come talk to her. A few moments later, we heard a man's voice come through the spirit box.

"Marci, I'm here," it said, as clear as day.

The spirit of Marci's father spoke to her about a boat, which seemed to strike a chord with her. He told her that he loved her and that he would always be with her. Although she cried, they were tears of relief and joy. It was amazing to see the emotional healing manifest within her as she spoke with her father, having missed the chance to do so before he transitioned. After his energy left the room, Marci and I went outside together and she told me why her father's words had so clearly impacted her. She was scheduled the next day to go out on a boat and spread his ashes on a lake.

On another occasion, a man named Russell wanted to communicate with his deceased best friend. We did a session to contact him using Steven Huff's portal.

"Scott, are you with me? Can we talk?" Russell asked as we began. "I want to know that you're okay."

A voice answered with Russell's first and last names, confirming it was indeed his best friend. They talked for a bit, mostly about being truck drivers. It was clear that this conversation meant a lot to Russell. Although he was a very alpha male, tears sprang into his eyes as he spoke. I still keep in contact with Russell and his wife to this day. I find it comforting and a little ironic how many friends I've made through the afterlife.

One woman drove all the way from Massachusetts, a trip of over ten hours, to communicate with her deceased husband. The communication was successful and, afterward, she asked if she could stay at the house for a few days, because she felt that his presence was still there. When I told her that someone would have to stay with her, she readily agreed. I left Steven Huff's portal with her so that she could continue to talk to her husband through it. After she left, I went to clean up the house and found that she had left us metaphysical presents as thanks. She also sent me a handwritten note to tell me how much she had appreciated being able to connect with her husband. She said that it changed her life and that, since then, she'd felt so much peace.

Although physical healings are more visible to the naked eye and are often viewed as both shocking and miraculous, I find something equally miraculous in the emotional healing that can come from being able to communicate with those we've lost. I'm very glad that Bellaire House has allowed so many people to gain that peace over the years. And I feel very lucky to have witnessed it.

HELPFUL HINTS

While it may not be able to heal your physical wounds, a healing bath is something you can use to speed emotional healing, to remove lingering negative energy, and to provide a spiritual balm to your soul. Run a bath and make sure that the water is a comfortable temperature—don't make it hotter or colder than you like. Add skin-friendly herbs or essential oils like lavender or chamomile to the water. And don't forget the kosher salt. In addition to being spiritually purifying, salt is a natural disinfectant that can keep small physical wounds clean and free of infection.

Relax in your healing bath and let the water carry away any negative energy or emotions. You will feel refreshed and renewed afterward. For an added boost of power, fill a cut-crystal bottle with spring water and allow it to charge in the sun or moonlight. Just make sure you leave the bottle to charge in a safe place where it won't pick up any negative energy from the surroundings. You can also light candles or incense to enhance your healing bath, but remember to put them in a safe place so they don't become fire hazards.

A Completion

After all of the darkness we've explored in this book—all the negative energy and malign intent that lurks in every shadowy corner of Bellaire House, in the attic, in the depths of the basement—I thought it would be nice to end on a positive note. So here's a story with a happy ending. In fact, this is a true tale of the most profound thing that ever happened to me as the owner of a haunted house.

It was a Full Blue Moon on New Year's Eve—the first "Super-Blood Blue Moon" in more than 150 years. The lunar energy is extremely powerful and very long-lasting during a moon phase like this, so it was the perfect time to host a public paranormal investigation at Bellaire House. Maria Schmidt, founder of National Ghost Hunting Day and one of my favorite investigators, and my friend Mike Simpson were with me to welcome our guests. As the night wore on, we conducted a spiritual communication session in the attic, where we made contact with a spirit who told us his name was Gary. He claimed to have been a servant who worked for the Heatherington family.

Gary described himself as being twenty-seven years old and originally from Florida. He told us that he and three of his friends had taken shelter in the attic's cubbyhole because they were hiding from a very negative force that lived deep in the crevices of the house. This was very likely the malevolent entity with whom we were already familiar. Gary said that this dark force was extremely malicious and violent, and that his four-year-old son had been manipulated by it, causing him to open an attic window, step out, and plunge to his death. He also told us that his wife was somewhere in the house, but that he could not find her. She had apparently died there of depression, broken-hearted over the death of their son.

The message we received from Gary was one of the most intense spiritual communications we had ever collected. We captured it on both video and audio recordings. Moreover, many parts of Gary's story struck a personal chord with me. He mentioned that he and his friends were hiding in the attic's cubby-hole, a place that I and several other researchers had long suspected was once used to hide escaped slaves as they traveled the Underground Railroad. This tracked with Gary's claim that he was originally from Florida. We also know that the attic has a long and troubling history. *Something* there seems repeatedly to manipulate residents into jumping out of its gable windows. I began to wonder if Gary's son was the servant's child rumored to have fallen to its death from those windows and if that incident had imprinted itself on the house at a psychic level.

Bellaire House can, in fact, get fixated on certain events in time. The more traumatizing an event, the more likely it is to leave a mark on the house's nature—sometimes a mark so deep that it is almost physical. The death of a child would certainly leave a scar. And I knew from my own personal encounters with the malicious and violent entity that dwelled in the attic that the house harbored violent and traumatizing energies. So my heart went out to the spirit of Gary and the idea of someone waiting, trapped in that dark attic cubbyhole, alone with the house's evil entity.

Perhaps that's why, at the peak of the session's energy, I did the worst thing that any paranormal investigator can ever do. I told Gary's spirit that it could use my energy to reach out. I knew in my head that this was wrong, but my heart was so immersed in what Gary was telling us that I became very emotional and I let my guard down. Something told me that Gary was a good spirit and that I could trust him, so I threw the rule book out the window—metaphorically speaking. When Gary told us that he wasn't allowed to leave the attic, I told him that I owned the house, that it was the year 2018, and that he could roam around the house freely. He could sleep in the beds; he could eat the food. He was free and he was no longer a servant. I told him that, as the owner of the house, I was granting him his freedom in this dimension. I grabbed a piece of paper and hastily wrote: "Gary, you are free." Then I signed my name and left the paper in the cubbyhole in the attic. When Mike Simpson firmly told me that I was putting everyone present in danger and that I needed to take a break, I snapped back to myself and realized what I'd done. Mike was correct; it had been incredibly risky behavior on my part—something I would never recommend that another paranormal investigator do.

About a month after the spiritual communication session with Gary, as I was enjoying a day in my own home, I was surprised when the doorbell rang. I wasn't expecting anyone. I opened the door to find a black man standing there with a phone in his hand. After I greeted him, he introduced himself as Gary and said that he was sorry to intrude, but that he wanted to inquire about the apartment for rent below mine. He told me that he and his wife were expecting their first child and that she was currently a patient at the OBGYN next door. They were looking for a new home. I took down Gary's name and phone number and, while he stood there, texted them to my landlord to let him know that there was an inquiry about the apartment. My landlord quickly responded and said he would set up a meeting that day. I passed the information on to Gary, then bid him goodbye. By that time, it was late in the afternoon and Layne had just come home from school; we were in a rush to get him to his bowling practice.

Then the doorbell rang again. When I opened the front door, there stood Gary, this time with a beautiful and clearly pregnant woman whom I took to be his wife. When I asked how I could help him, he replied that he was waiting for maintenance to show him the apartment. I thought that he might have gotten lost, so I offered to show him where the apartment entrance was and suggested that he wait for maintenance there.

As we walked around to the entry to the apartment below mine, Gary looked me in the eyes and said something that thoroughly confused me in the moment. "Kristin Lee," he said, "my family is eternally grateful for what you have done for us." At the time, I didn't understand his meaning at all. I thought that I had just helped him inquire about an apartment and shown him around to the entrance. I was just being friendly, doing what any good prospective neighbor would do. Confused but touched, I told Gary and his wife that, if it worked out and they moved in, we could have a barbecue on the back porch one day. They held hands and smiled at me, and Gary thanked me a few more times as we said our goodbyes. I felt a bit odd, but mostly excited. I liked the couple and hoped they got the apartment. Besides, I thought it would be nice to have a baby in the house.

It wasn't until later that afternoon, as I was driving Layne to his bowling practice, that I was struck by a realization that hit me like a bolt of lightning. I felt as if I had been electrified, and I knew in my heart that the Gary I had just met was the spirit we'd encountered in the Bellaire House attic. I didn't know how it could be possible, but I felt in my bones that it was true. If you've ever had an epiphany—a true and powerful epiphany that makes you feel as if you've been granted information from a higher power—then you know how absolutely stunned I was. In fact, I had to pull over. After all, the road is not the best place in the world to realize that somehow you've just encountered a spirit from your haunted house—in the flesh! I needed to take a deep breath and look at the situation logically.

Perhaps most important, I knew I needed to look at my phone. I had taken down Gary's phone number to text to my landlord. If it had really happened, there would be a record on my phone—a record of the text I had sent. Did I really send that message or had I been dreaming? Was I delusional? Had Bellaire House, which for years and years had tried to wear me down spiritually and psychologically, finally pushed me over the edge? Or had there been some sort of slip in time—a kind of psychological or spiritual dislocation? Chills ran up and down my entire body. Even though, in my heart, I knew what I had experienced, I was assailed by denial and disbelief. But somehow I just *knew* that Gary was the spirit from the attic in the flesh. I knew it with the kind of bone-deep certainty that most people go their entire lifetimes without feeling. The emotions were so overwhelming that, in that moment, I felt as if all my senses had gone numb, as if I'd gone into shock. As I slowly came back to myself, all I could hear was my son complaining that he was going to be late.

Somehow, under the dire threat of making my teenager late for bowling practice, I managed to pull myself together enough so that I could drive. I put my thoughts about Gary on hold long enough to get Layne to the bowling alley. As soon as he got out of the car, however, I pulled over in the parking lot to see if my phone actually contained a phone number that I had texted to my landlord, and whether or not it had a Florida area code. I scrolled through my texts until I found the number and then immediately Googled the area code. It was a Florida code. I sat there stunned, staring at my phone. What were the chances? What were the odds?

I called Maria and Mike, who had been present when we made contact with Gary's spirit in the attic and told them what had transpired. They were completely bowled over. They said that it was a completion! We think that, after our communication session, Gary's spirit found the strength to leave the attic and found his wife's soul somewhere in the house. Then they left together. We think they had been caught in some kind of time warp, trapped between two or more dimensions. When they escaped, they were finally able to find freedom and be reborn into a world of peace and happiness with their child.

As the years have passed and as it's become clear that I will continue to own Bellaire House, my biggest fear has become that I may be trapped in the house after I transition to spirit. The house and I are connected, whether I like it or not, and I have seen what happens to those who are connected with it. Lyde, Edwin, Eliza, Emily, Mary, the Gray Man, the servants—they all resided, at one point or another, in the house and that is where their spirits remain now. I don't want to meet the same fate—tied to Bellaire House and under the control of the malevolent entity that dwells within it. Gary's story is comforting to me because he and his wife were able to leave the house and start over. Gary was even able to come to me to let me know that he was okay. I'll always treasure that memory, as well as the incredibly profound experience of getting to see Gary in the flesh. So, while I am happy for Gary and his wife, I am happy for myself as well. At least I know of one happy ending in Bellaire House.

About the Author

Kristin Lee is the proprietor of the Bellaire House Research Center, a mental health professional, and psychic medium who specializes in overcoming demonic entities. Visit her at *thebellairehouse.webs.com.*